Learning to Weather the Storm

A Story of Life, Love, and Alzheimer's

Lauren Dykovitz

ISBN-13: 978-1545484487
ISBN-10: 1545484481

For you, Mom.

Here Comes the Rain

It's hard to pinpoint now exactly when it all started. I think it slowly crept in on us the way a thunderstorm often does on a hot and hazy summer afternoon. It's up there, overhead, lingering in the dark clouds, but you don't realize that it's there until the rain hits you. Maybe my mom knew it was happening long before any of the rest of us. Maybe she realized that she was forgetting things more often than normal. Maybe she was even afraid. I wish that I would have thought to ask her back then. Now, there is no way to get an answer from her. The disease has already stolen most of her mind.

I think that somewhere deep down inside, I knew what was happening. It was more than just the occasional lapse of memory or forgetting someone's name, which she did often. My mom would ask the same question repeatedly during a conversation. I initially thought that she was repeating the question because she had forgotten my answer or simply wasn't paying attention to me when I had responded. I would always snap at her and tell her to pay attention so that I didn't have to repeat myself all the time. Over time, I began to realize that she was repeating the same question because she had completely forgotten that she had already asked it. She also forgot the small details of my life. I was a police officer at the time. She always forgot what shift I was working that week or what days I had off, regardless of the fact that I reminded her constantly. These were things that anyone could easily forget, given the hustle and bustle of day to day life. So, I thought that some of her forgetfulness was probably normal, justified. But, it was more than just forgetting that she had asked me a question or forgetting my response to it. She was forgetting much more. Things that I could not justify how she had forgotten them. Things that raised big, huge, red flags in my mind.

My mom had ordered unsweetened iced tea at restaurants for literally my entire life. She had always used two Sweet-n-Lows and a lemon to fix her tea. My sister, Melissa, and I noticed immediately when she began to forget how to fix it. She would ask one of us what she used. One time, she started putting salt in her iced tea instead of sugar or sweetener. Surely, this could have been an innocent mistake. However, my mom didn't recognize her mistake. It was like she thought putting salt in her iced tea was completely normal. When Melissa and I pointed out her mistake, she seemed embarrassed, flustered, and completely unaware of her own error. She would just laugh it off like it was no big deal. How in the world could she forget how to do something that she did so frequently? I mean, fixing her iced tea was something that she had always done instinctively, without even having to think about the process. This was one of the things that raised a big red flag for me. It was no longer just forgetting facts, names, and information. It had become forgetting how to do things that she had done every day throughout her whole life.

Other than forgetting information and how to do things, my mom seemed to be struggling significantly with her vision. She had always worn glasses for reading and distance, but this was different. My mom would take her glasses off and put them on the kitchen counter. When she needed them again, she couldn't remember where she had put them, so she would ask me where her glasses were. I would tell her that they were on the kitchen counter, right in front of her. My mom still couldn't find them, so she would ask again. I would point directly to her glasses with my finger, sometimes even putting my hand on top of them, to show her where they were. My mom would touch the kitchen counter space to the left or right of her glasses, but she was never able to place her hand directly on top of her glasses. She would tap her hand all along the bare kitchen counter without being able to land on her glasses. Finally, I would take her hand and put it on top of her glasses for her. Only then was she able to find her glasses. My mom did this with several other things, as well. She was unable to find the phone, the remote, her drink, a light switch on the wall, and even the doorknob on any given door. I found this to be very troubling. I mean, it was one thing to have blurred vision and to need glasses for reading or driving, but it was quite another to not be able to see an object that was literally right in front of her face, even after someone had pointed directly to it. It was as if everything blended in together. Nothing popped out. Nothing appeared to be three-dimensional to her. I had absolutely no reason or justification for her vision problems.

My mom exhibited a few other odd behaviors for which I had no explanation. Whenever I went over to her house, I noticed little notes posted throughout the house. Some of the notes were simple reminders to herself about appointments, things she needed to do, or the times/channels of television shows that she wanted to watch. I didn't find the notes themselves all that strange. It was the fact that I never remembered my mom having the need to make notes like these in the past. That was what sort of bothered me. My mom also posted notes all over the house about their cat, Ravyn. She began to keep Ravyn in Melissa's old bedroom with the door closed. She never let Ravyn out of that room for fear that she would somehow get out of the house and go missing. My mom left notes all over the house to remind everyone, and perhaps herself, that there was a cat in that bedroom and not to let her out of the room. I actually still have one of the notes that I found lying around their house years ago. I found this sudden obsession with Ravyn getting out of the house to be very troubling. No incident had occurred to spark this obsession. It just started out of the clear blue sky one day.

In addition, I began to notice certain personality changes in my mom. She had always been a chatty Cathy. She was always very talkative and social. She would talk to the cashier at the grocery store all the time, to the point where they knew quite a bit about each other's lives and families. My mom could strike up a conversation with a complete stranger while waiting in line somewhere. She probably could have held a meaningful conversation with a brick wall. She was just that type of person. She always had something to say and she was always chattering away. I remember her talking to strangers so much that it actually used to annoy and embarrass me at times. At some point, she had become less talkative and less social. She didn't have as much to say and she started to become withdrawn from certain conversations and social interactions.

I remember one specific incident that really stood out to me. In March of 2010, my boyfriend (now husband), Steve, and I were moving from one apartment to another. My parents, sister, and brother-in-law were all with us at our new apartment, helping us move in and unpack. Normally, my mom would have been a big help with carrying things into the apartment and helping me unpack boxes. She would have helped me organize things and get settled in, like she did when I had moved in 2009. However, on this occasion, I remember her sitting on the floor in our bare living room, completely withdrawn and helpless. She just sat there watching all of us move into the apartment. It was like she had no idea what to do with herself or how to interact with us. She didn't know how to help anymore. She just sat there, staring at the wall, waiting for us to finish. It was the strangest thing and very unusual for my mom to act this way. Even more unusual was the fact that she seemed to blame all of us, thinking that we had been excluding and ignoring her. She was upset with all of us for leaving her out while we were all busy moving and unpacking. She didn't even realize that she had been excluding herself from the group. I remember being concerned about her strange behavior back then, but I had no idea what it meant.

I wish I could remember more of the obvious signs that something was really wrong with my mom. It seems like so long ago now and so much has happened since then. All I know is that when I added them all up, I definitely knew that *something* was wrong. We could no longer pass her behavior off as quirky or ditzy, like we had done in the past. Still, it wasn't really enough for me to be absolutely certain of *what* was wrong with my mom. I think that somewhere in the back of my mind I knew what it could be, but I wasn't about to readily admit it to myself or anyone else. Something was wrong and there had to be an explanation for all of her odd behaviors, but what? I still didn't think that it was enough to warrant a visit to the doctor. After all, she was completely healthy other than her strange behaviors and forgetfulness. I really didn't know what to do about it.

But then, one day it hit me. Just like that afternoon thunderstorm on a hot and hazy summer day. The rain drops began to fall. I remember it so well. I was home in my apartment on a day off from work. My mom called me. She was upset and said that she had just gotten into a minor car accident. I asked her to tell me what had happened. She said that she had gone to the grocery store, Giant, and was on her way home. She was driving along the road on which her neighborhood was located. She said that she suddenly forgot where she was and almost missed the turn into her neighborhood. She instinctively slammed on her brakes in order to avoid missing the turn. The car behind her did not have enough room to stop and it ran right into the back of her car. A minor fender bender. No damage. No injuries. No big deal, right? Wrong. I freaked out. What did she mean that she suddenly forgot where she was and almost missed the turn into her own neighborhood? She had only been living in that neighborhood for about twenty years. She probably went to Giant a few times a week. This errand and the route she took were definitely nothing new to her. How could she just simply forget a routine that was so familiar to her?

I was glad that she was uninjured, but I was still very concerned. I became more concerned when she told me that the other driver had claimed to have neck pain and asked for her insurance information. The concern grew even more when she told me that she had given him her information, but that she did not ask for his in return. What?! I was a police officer for god's sake! How could she not have asked for his information? I could have at least called him to explain the situation. Luckily, we never heard from the other driver and nothing ever came of this seemingly minor accident. However, it raised yet another big red flag in my mind. Now, my mom's odd behavior was putting her safety at risk. What if nearly missing the turn into her neighborhood had caused a much bigger accident? What if she was killed? What if she had killed someone else? I knew that something was definitely wrong. Something had to be done.

I talked to Melissa about all of the changes that we had been noticing in our mom. It seemed as if the rain had begun to fall harder and we could see that a storm was approaching. We decided to talk to our dad and suggested that our mom see a doctor. Naturally, they were both very resistant. They kept telling us that nothing was wrong and that there was no need to see a doctor. My mom just kept saying that she was just getting older. However, at the time, she was only 62 years old and I hardly thought that her memory loss was consistent with normal aging. Both of my parents basically told us that it really wasn't any of our business. The two of them talked about it privately and decided that they would handle it, whatever *it* was, on their own. I remember talking to my mom about it on the phone. She said, "We're going to take care of it." I said, "What do you mean?" And she replied, "Your father and I will take care of it by ourselves. Just the two of us." She became upset when I started to push the issue and question why Melissa and I were being left out of the whole thing. I think she even started to ask my dad to come to the phone to talk to me about it. My parents were always of the opinion that their business was their business and their problems were their problems. They always handled everything quietly by themselves, without involving anyone else in the matter. And, they had always treated Melissa and I like we were just children and nothing was ever any of our business. That's just the way it had always been. Old school. Why did I expect this situation to be any different?

I don't remember all of the details surrounding her doctor visits and the timeline of it all, but I do remember that it took quite a lot of convincing before my parents would even consider seeing a doctor. When they finally made an appointment, neither of my parents told us anything about it, until after the fact. My parents said that my mom's primary care physician had diagnosed her with anxiety and prescribed her with Xanax. They had a "see, we told you it wasn't anything serious" attitude about the whole thing. Like, since they had seen a doctor and been given a blanket diagnosis, that was the end of it.

I was pretty sure that my parents had not been completely honest with the doctor about my mom's symptoms, which most likely led to a misdiagnosis of anxiety. My mom began taking Xanax as it was prescribed to her. However, the Xanax made my mom very drowsy and tired. She was napping almost every time I called her or went to the house to see her. I didn't like it and neither did Melissa. Plus, my mom was still having problems with her memory and vision. The problem was far from being solved. Melissa and I both agreed that our parents were probably not completely honest with the doctor. We had a feeling that they had withheld significant information because they were afraid of what might actually be going on. I mean, who could blame them? We weren't happy with the diagnosis that our mom had been given and we felt obligated to look further into it. There had to be more that we could do. We begged. We pleaded. We wouldn't back down, until my parents agreed to revisit the doctor.

From what I can remember, my mom initially contacted her primary care physician again and was referred to see a neurologist. My parents went to the first appointment with the neurologist by themselves. They told us that the neurologist had administered some tests and that he agreed with the initial diagnosis of anxiety. He wanted my mom to continue taking Xanax and to return to him for a follow-up visit in a couple of months. No, no, no! I couldn't believe this bullshit. Now, not one, but two doctors had misdiagnosed her with anxiety. I realized that I couldn't place all of the blame on the doctors for the misdiagnosis. I wasn't even sure if it was their fault at all. But, I was definitely blaming my parents. I was pissed at them because I was absolutely certain that they were not being completely honest with these doctors.

I don't remember exactly how much time had gone by, but I think it had been a couple of months or so. Melissa and I had insisted on going to the next doctor's appointment with our parents, so that we could be sure that they were being completely honest about all of my mom's symptoms. I remember how nervous we all were, especially my poor mom. We all sat in the doctor's office, as Melissa and I told him all of our concerns about my mom. How humiliated and ashamed my mom must have been! The doctor seemed surprised to hear some of what we had to say, which further convinced me that my parents had not been completely honest with him. The doctor said that he was going to re-test my mom. He gave her the same tests that he had given her at the first appointment. They consisted of only a few questions, which included remembering a list of words and replicating a drawing. My mom had a lot of trouble with the drawing. It was a three-dimensional drawing, but she drew it as two separate two-dimensional drawings, side by side. It was as if she wasn't seeing it correctly. I initially thought that this meant that my mom was having problems with her vision. It made sense considering all of the difficulties she had been having with seeing things that were right in front of her. I didn't realize that it really meant that although my mom's eyes and vision were fine, her brain was having trouble recognizing what her eyes were seeing. We left the doctor's office that day without any new information. My mom was to receive some additional testing, and be seen by her eye doctor, before the neurologist made an official determination. I don't remember all of the exact details, but I do remember when the storm finally hit.

I was working the day shift, with about an hour left to go, when I got a call from my mom. She was upset and said that she had heard back from the neurologist. After the additional testing and further speaking with my mom, the neurologist had changed his original diagnosis of anxiety to Alzheimer's disease. Fucking Alzheimer's. It hit me like a bolt of lightning. I saw that the dark clouds had been closing in. I felt the drops of rain hitting my skin. Somewhere, in the back of my mind, I knew what was coming. But, the loud roar of the thunder still made me jump. Just like the thunderstorm. I knew it was there, hovering over our heads, but I almost didn't believe it, until it finally hit me. I don't know what I said to my mom after she told me. I was in shock and disbelief. I couldn't think. I couldn't breathe. And, I sure as shit couldn't finish my shift.

The first thing I did when I hung up the phone was call my supervisor. I told him that I was upset because I had just received some bad news about my mom's health. He didn't even hesitate before telling me to go home. He even told me to call out sick the next day if I felt like I needed more time. Done and done. I went home immediately and called my then boyfriend/fiancé, Steve. (Oddly enough, I got engaged that same month. I can't for the life of me remember which happened first, but they both occurred in July 2010.) He was also a police officer and his shift ended an hour before mine, so he met me at our apartment. I cried and cried. It felt as though there had been a death in the family. But, no one had died. I didn't know what to do with myself. I was so upset and I didn't know where to go from there. What was I supposed to do for the rest of the day? Or the next day? Or any day from then on? It was like a punch to the gut. A knife in my heart. The rug had been pulled right out from underneath me. My whole world turned upside down. I felt lost. Completely and utterly lost.

I went to my parents' house that night. It felt as if we were meeting to grieve the loss of a loved one. Everyone was so sad and no one knew what to do next. I mean, there really wasn't anything we could do. No funeral services to be planned. No eulogy to be written. No pictures to gather for a slideshow. There had not been a death. No surgeries to be scheduled. No treatments to begin. No fighting to commence. There was not a cure. When my mom found a lump in her breast, she had surgery to remove it. When she found out that it was breast cancer, she had chemotherapy and radiation to treat it. A few years later, she was cured from breast cancer. It was gone. Done and over with. She moved on with her life. This was different. There were no surgeries or treatments to cure Alzheimer's. There was nothing to schedule. Nothing to do. Except wait. Sit back and wait for this horrific disease to destroy her mind and our lives.

What does one do with this information? It's not even as if she had been diagnosed with a terminal illness. Well, Alzheimer's ultimately is terminal and she would eventually die from it. But, someday, not today. In some ways, I thought that it would have been easier to digest the diagnosis of a terminal illness. At least then we would have had an end in sight. Somewhere to go from there. Closure. Alzheimer's is like being sentenced to life in prison for a crime you didn't commit. Only you wake up each morning forgetting where you are and why you're there. So, you just sit and wait for the disease to take hold of your mind and control of your life. You are helpless against it. There is nothing you can do to get rid of it or to speed up the process. The only thing you can do is wait for it to kill you. And, only then, will you feel relief from its chokehold. It is like sitting in a prison cell, waiting to die. You are trapped inside of your own mind and death is your only escape. And so, the question remained, where did we go from there?

I called out of work the day after my mom received her diagnosis. I went out to lunch with my mom and Melissa, like we had done many times before. We just wanted to spend some time with our mom and try to get a handle on her diagnosis. However, it was different now. It was *after*. My life would now forever be divided into two categories: *before* and *after*. *Before* my mom was diagnosed with Alzheimer's. *After* my mom was diagnosed with Alzheimer's. Her life and the lives of all of those who loved her would now be forever marked by this disease. To look at us having lunch that day, it seemed as though nothing had changed. But, to step back and take a look at the big picture, everything had changed. There was now a big, dark cloud hanging over our heads. A long, winding road, full of peaks and valleys, that lay open in front of us. A future unknown to us, but already predetermined by my mom's illness. The only thing that was certain to any of us was that there would be a lot of pain and suffering, tears, and hard work in the days to come. But, on that day, we were just three girls having lunch at Panera. Each of us trying to summon the strength and courage that we would need to move on with our lives and deal with the hand that we had just been dealt.

A couple of days after my mom received her diagnosis, I told my best friend. She really didn't know what to say to comfort me. There really wasn't anything that she could say. Her only experience with Alzheimer's was that her grandmother had died from it. In that moment, I realized that I would be completely alone in my struggle. At least, that's how it felt at the time. I was only 25 years old and my mom, who was only 62 years old, had just been diagnosed with Alzheimer's. Not my grandmother. My mother. The woman who had raised me and had become my friend in my adult life. No one my age was ever going to understand what I was going through. It was completely different to have a grandparent with Alzheimer's than it was to have a parent with Alzheimer's, especially at my age. I had no one to talk to who actually understood what I was going through. No one to give me advice or comfort. The only person I knew who was in the same situation as me was Melissa. But, I felt as though I couldn't talk to her about it. Every time I was upset about our mom and turned to her for comfort, I ended up comforting her instead. I found myself sugar-coating it for her. Making it seem like it wasn't as bad or like I wasn't as upset as I really was. I never wanted to bring it up to her because I thought that it would only upset her. Talking to her about our mom wasn't going to make me feel any better and it was going to make her feel worse. So, what was the point? The only other people who could have possibly understood my pain were much older than me. Most people who had a parent with Alzheimer's were much older than I was at the time of my mom's diagnosis. And, I didn't even know anyone who had a parent with Alzheimer's anyway. I had never felt so alone. So very lost and so very alone. I had plenty of shoulders to cry on, but none of them would understand my tears.

In the beginning, I only told Steve and my best friend that my mom had been diagnosed with Alzheimer's. My mom and dad told our family members and Melissa told some of our mutual friends. I think Steve told his family and my best friend told some of our other friends. But, I told no one. It had nothing to do with being ashamed or being in denial. I just felt like no one could possibly ever understand or appreciate the impact that my mom's diagnosis had on me. I also didn't want to make anyone uncomfortable by talking about it. No one would know how to respond or what to say to me. Honestly, there was a good chance that no matter what they said to me, I would take it the wrong way and it would just piss me off. No one would have any experience to draw from. No one would know how to deal with my situation or my feelings. Everyone would be completely uncomfortable. Plus, I have never been the type of person to call my friends up to bitch and complain about my problems. If someone had asked me about my problems, I would have been more likely to talk about them. But, in this case, no one was asking because no one knew that anything was wrong. And, no one knew because, again, I'm not the type of person to go on and on about my problems. I felt like bringing it up would only make people feel uncomfortable because they wouldn't know how to deal with it. That was the last thing that I wanted to do. And, I had it ingrained in my mind that no one would even care that my mom had Alzheimer's. At the time, she seemed almost completely normal to outsiders. I felt like people would think that there was nothing wrong with her and that I was being overly dramatic about her condition. I felt like no one really wanted to hear it. I mean, it wasn't like she had died. Then, people might care. I always reminded myself that there were many people who had it far worse than me, so I had no right to complain about my problems. Besides, nobody liked a Debbie Downer. My friends were all out trying to soak up their mid-twenties and relive their college days. Everyone was just trying to have a good time. I didn't want them to be like, "Oh god, here comes Lauren again, talking about the Alzheimer's." I didn't want to be the one bringing everyone down and making everyone feel depressed. I just felt like no one would care. They wouldn't get it. No one wanted to hear it.

So, I just shut down. I didn't tell anyone. I didn't talk about it. I didn't read about it. Maybe I was in denial, but, then again, I knew exactly what was going on. Maybe I was just trying to avoid reality. I didn't have the tools that I needed to cope with and accept my mom's Alzheimer's, so I just avoided it. I kept everything bottled up inside of me, not wanting to bother anyone else with my problems. I cringed anytime anyone asked me about my mom. I would just say that she was doing ok. Hanging in there. No one really wanted to hear the awful truth. The details of her illness. No one wanted to deal with the reality of it all. No one actually cared. They just wanted to hear that she was doing ok, so that's what I told them. I never went into detail. I didn't want to talk about it. I didn't want to make anyone uncomfortable. I didn't want to burden anyone with my problems, especially since they couldn't relate to them anyway. I didn't know the damage that I was doing to myself by holding it all in. To my heart. To my soul. To my relationship with Steve. I was about to embark on a long, emotional, rollercoaster of a journey. The journey of planning my wedding without the mother of the bride.

A Motherless Bride

Time moved on, as it always does. I was busy working a crazy ass job with crazy ass hours. I was up overnight and trying to sleep during the day. My weekends were often Tuesday, Wednesday, and Thursday. My Monday's often fell on a Saturday. I felt completely cut off from the outside world. The real world. I existed in a bubble that consisted only of police work and other police officers. I fucking hated it. I hated everything and everyone. All of my time off was spent trying to catch up on sleep, housework, errands, and chores. Plus, I became immersed in wedding planning. The venue, the dress, the flowers, the food, the music, the photographer, and all of that other bullshit that you spend a small fortune on for the quickest, shortest day of your entire life. I barely had time to call my mom, let alone stop by her house to see her. I would become frustrated when talking to her about my wedding because she would forget everything I told her anyway. She wasn't able to appreciate the fact that her youngest daughter was getting married. She was so involved in planning Melissa's wedding, which was in 2006. That was all I ever wanted for my own wedding. I wanted my mom to surprise me by buying me something for the wedding. A "soon-to-be Mrs. Dykovitz" zip-up hooded sweatshirt like she had gotten for Melissa. I wanted her to go to bridal shows and appointments with me. I wanted her to help me pick out our save-the-dates and invitations. I wanted her to be present in the moment, not just physically, but mentally and emotionally, as well. I wanted her to acknowledge the fact that I was getting married and that it was a big deal. Just as big of a deal as when Melissa got married.

I tried to include her in as much as possible, but, sometimes it was honestly just easier to do things without her. Taking her to an appointment with me would require too much of an explanation and would cause me too much stress. I was stressed out enough as it was. And, to be completely honest, I was often embarrassed by her behavior around strangers. It wasn't yet obvious that there was something wrong with my mom, so people who didn't know any better probably just thought she was weird. I'm ashamed to admit that I was ever embarrassed by her behavior, but I was. I tried to include her as much as possible, but most of the time I just didn't feel like dealing with it. Harsh, but true.

Since all of my bridesmaids were working when I was off and were off when I was working, I ended up doing 99% of everything that needed to be done by myself. I even ordered my own "soon-to-be Mrs. Dykovitz" zip-up hooded sweatshirt. How fucking sad is that? I picked out almost everything by myself. Well, at least everything that Steve showed absolutely no interest in helping me pick out. Steve and I took our parents along with us to look at wedding venues one day, but we couldn't decide on one that day. We ended up picking a venue that we went to look at by ourselves. I picked out the save-the-dates, the invitations, the string quartet, the DJ, the photographer, the flowers. You name it, I picked it out. I didn't have my mom's opinion or advice on anything, but I guess that could have been a good thing. I did all the work and all the planning all by myself.

I invited everyone to go with me when I tried on wedding dresses. I felt like I had to include everyone so that no one felt left out. My mom came along, but it was clear to me that she did not fully understand or appreciate what we were doing there that day. It was like she just thought that I was trying on any old dress. She didn't have a huge smile on her face or tears of joy in her eyes. She wasn't excited. Instead, she had a far-away glance in her eyes and it felt as if she wasn't even there at all. She seemed lost and confused. She was withdrawn. She just sat there.

I guess I expected some big reaction out of everyone when I found THE dress. When I didn't get that reaction, I was hugely disappointed. My mom didn't really have much of a reaction at all. She just looked at me in every dress like it was just a dress. Like I was just some girl. Everyone else just kept saying that it was up to me to decide. Meanwhile, I was thinking, "No, god dammit! Everyone better start fucking crying right now and tell me how fucking beautiful I look. Tell me which dress I'm supposed to pick!" Maybe I was over-reacting, but I wanted some feel-good story about the day that I found my wedding dress. You know, "It was magical. I walked out in THE dress. My mom looked at me and started crying. I started crying. We hugged. We laughed. We all cried." There was none of that. My mom just kept looking at me like, "Are we done yet?"

I realized that my wedding was going to be very different from my sister's wedding. I decided that, for my own sanity, I wouldn't invite my mom to every single wedding planning appointment. I wanted to be able to say that I had included her in some things though, so I took her to my appointment with the florist. She had no clue where we were or what we were doing. She kept talking to the florist like he was an old friend of hers and he kept looking at her like she was bat shit crazy. But, we got through the appointment, picked out my flowers, and it made me feel better to have included her in something. And so, the planning continued.

Just in case we didn't have enough on our plates already, Steve and I decided to start house-hunting just a couple of months into planning our wedding. The lease on our apartment was going to be up in a few months and I really wanted to come home to a house after our honeymoon, instead of just an apartment. We must have looked at twenty houses or more before we finally found the right one. We really liked a few of the houses we looked at and even put an offer in on one, but it didn't work out. My mom's Alzheimer's definitely played a huge part in choosing our new home. I knew that I didn't want to live too far away from her and my dad. I wanted to be close enough that I could run over to their house with a moment's notice in case my mom needed something. I knew that my parents would never just come over to our house without calling first, so that would never be an issue. We also wanted to be close to work so that we didn't have a long drive home after working a 10+ hour shift. We found our house just before Christmas 2010. We made an offer on it and just like that, we bought a house. It was an early Christmas present to ourselves. I never thought that I would be the type of person to live so close to my parents. I always thought that I might end up in a different state from them. But, Alzheimer's had definitely changed all of that. The house we bought was just over two miles away from my parents' house.

Along with buying a house came another to-do list, in addition to our ever-growing wedding to-do list, and there was still that god-awful job that I hated. Steve had promised to take care of all the house stuff, since I was taking care of all of the wedding stuff. The time flew by and, before I knew it, it was February 2011 and we were moving into our new house. There were a few things that we wanted done to the house before we actually moved into it. We hired a painter to paint most of the rooms and we had carpet installed in most of the rooms, as well. We ended up hiring movers to move us in. True to our nature, we did most of the work by ourselves. Neither of us liked to ask anyone for help. Given that Steve's parents lived in New Jersey and my parents were busy dealing with my mom's Alzheimer's, we didn't feel right asking them for help. Plus, they had already helped us move at least five times in the past. None of our friends were available when we were available either, so it was just the two of us. In no time at all, we were settled into our new house, where we would become husband and wife.

I remember the first time my mom came over to see our new house. She seemed so confused. She shuffled around our house like it was a stranger's house. She didn't even take off her coat. She couldn't help me decorate, unpack, or organize any of the rooms. She didn't understand what a big deal it was that we had just bought our first house. It was all lost on her. Before my mom had Alzheimer's, she would have gotten us a nice housewarming gift and made a big deal about our first house. Things were different now. She had no clue where our house was or that it was only about two miles away from her own house. It could have been in another country for all she knew. Once she was diagnosed with Alzheimer's, her doctor told us that she could no longer drive. I had once dreamed of the day when my mom would drive over to my house to pick me up and we would go out to lunch. Well, that was never going to happen now. To be honest, I don't even think she liked being at my house. It was strange to her. It was unfamiliar. I always felt like she was uncomfortable being there. She never seemed to relax while she was there. She would sit down on the edge of the couch or the front stairs with her coat on like she couldn't wait to get out of there. She walked around my house like she was afraid to touch anything. She didn't act like a mother who was in her own daughter's house. She just seemed so uncomfortable being there. So far, owning a house was nothing like I had envisioned it to be. I was beginning to feel very sorry for myself.

Our house quickly became our home. We crossed things off of our wedding to-do list and added even more. In May 2011, I became a doggie mom for the first time. We adopted a black lab named Oakley. I would quickly discover that he was my soulmate and best friend. Well, aside from Steve, of course. But, I'll talk more about Oakley later. Time continued to fly by and the wedding countdown was on.

What was supposed to be the happiest time of my life was actually quite the opposite. I was an emotional wreck. I felt like I was on the verge of a mental breakdown every fucking day. All I did was cry. The only person who knew anything about it was Steve, my soon-to-be-husband. Lucky him. He was probably looking for a way out. I can vividly remember one day when I just sat on the floor in the laundry room with an enormous pile of dirty clothes and cried. I cried so hard I think I almost shit my pants. Steve just looked at me and said, "Do you think you'll ever be happy again?" And I just tried harder. Then he left and went to the gym. Not because he's an asshole, but because he just didn't know what to do. I was a hot mess. I was a ticking time bomb. I think he was afraid that if he touched me or said the wrong thing, I would explode.

Don't get me wrong, I was happy that we were getting married and I was excited about our wedding. It was just being drowned out with the pain, grief, and loneliness that I felt because of my mom's Alzheimer's. I can't even say that I was having a hard time coping. I was just simply NOT coping. Not at all. Not even a little bit. I still hadn't told very many people about my mom's diagnosis and I didn't talk to anyone about it, except for Steve. On top of that, I still hated my job. I hated who it made me as a person. It made me miserable, bitchy, and confrontational. It made me hate people and not want to deal with any of them. It made me anti-social, untrusting, and disgruntled. It was crushing my soul. It made me feel even more alone than I already felt. No one knew what I was going through or how I was feeling because I didn't tell anyone. I kept everything bottled up inside and I was about to explode.

I went through the motions of my bridal shower and my bachelorette party. Everything was perfect and I should have been so happy, but I wasn't. I just felt like I was pretending to enjoy it all. I felt like I was being fake all the time. Fake smile, fake laugh, and fake excitement over mixing bowls and baking sheets. I mean, don't get me wrong. I loved Steve and couldn't wait to call him my husband. But, I couldn't enjoy all of the wedding events because I felt like my mom wasn't really a part of any of it. She was there physically, but not mentally or emotionally. She was completely withdrawn and no longer able to join in with the group. She never remembered who anyone was or how we were related to them. I spent a lot of time explaining everything to her; what we were doing, who everyone was, and how they were related to her. She didn't understand what was going on. She just thought that someone was having a party. She had no idea that it was a wedding, let alone her own daughter's wedding. It felt like my mother's ghost was attending all of my wedding events. She was merely an empty shell of the mother who had raised me. She was an imposter. A phony. A fake. She wasn't my mom any more. I didn't know how to feel anything other than sad.

I imagine that many people would say that I was depressed. At times, I thought that maybe I *was* depressed. I had an overwhelming feeling of sadness, hopelessness, and loss. I had trouble finding happiness in anything, even in my upcoming wedding. I didn't enjoy doing things that had once made me happy. I felt like I didn't really fit in anywhere. I didn't feel comfortable being around anyone. I always felt like an outsider. I didn't feel like myself anymore. I didn't even know who I was. I was deeply sad, confused, hopeless, and overwhelmed. I missed my mom and the way things once were. I felt like I had been robbed of my time with her. Sure, we had spent plenty of time together, but it wasn't the same. It was never going to be the same again. Our adult relationship was nothing like I had ever imagined it to be. I had just started to appreciate my mom. I had just started to see her as more of a friend than a parent. We had just started to become friends and enjoy having girl time together. It seemed as though that was all taken away before it had really even begun. We were switching roles. I was becoming the mother and she was becoming the child. I was taking care of her instead of the other way around. I realized that this often happened in parent-child relationships, but it should not have been happening this soon. Not while I was in my mid-twenties. Although I didn't realize it at the time, I know now that all of my feelings could be attributed to the grieving process. I was grieving the loss of my mom, while she was still standing right in front of me.

I went through all of the five stages of grief. First, there was denial and isolation. I never thought it was possible for my mom to have Alzheimer's at her age. When she received an official diagnosis of Alzheimer's, I thought that if I denied it or ignored it, then it would go away. I didn't want to believe it, so I didn't. I completely isolated myself from anyone who might actually care about what I was going through. I didn't tell anyone about my mom's diagnosis except for Steve and one friend. No one at work knew that my mom had been diagnosed with Alzheimer's. I didn't tell any of my other friends or any family members. I didn't think that anyone would understand and I wasn't even willing to try. For me, I think denial and isolation went hand in hand. I thought that if I just avoided saying it out loud, then the whole thing would go away. Isolating myself from everyone allowed me to remain in denial. If I didn't tell anyone about it, then it must not be real.

Next, there was anger. I was angry and upset that my mom had Alzheimer's. She was such a good person and she definitely didn't deserve to be suffering from this disease. Still is and still doesn't. My mom had already battled breast cancer at age 49 and won. She had been through surgeries, chemotherapy, and radiation. Wasn't that enough? Did she really have to get Alzheimer's, too? I was so mad that this was happening to her, to us. Why did my mom have to get Alzheimer's at such a young age? Young for her at 62 and young for me at 25. Why did this disease have to take away the woman who raised me, just as we were starting to become friends? It just didn't seem fair. I wanted to grab Alzheimer's by the balls and twist so fucking hard that it would never mess with us again. I was just so angry.

Then, there was bargaining. In some ways, I blamed myself for my mom's Alzheimer's. I thought that she got sick because she spent most of her days at home by herself. My mom never worked a full-time job after Melissa and I were born. Once we were older and able to drive ourselves around, she spent most of her days at home, watching TV. I felt like I should have pushed her harder to go out and get a job or to at least volunteer somewhere. I felt like maybe if she had done something like that, then she wouldn't have gotten Alzheimer's. Over the years, Melissa and I had suggested to her several times that she find a job or volunteer at the hospital, but ultimately, it was my mom's decision not to work or volunteer. Still, I had convinced myself that I should have tried harder. It was all my fault. Or, maybe the stress that I caused her during my high school years was the reason that she got Alzheimer's. Maybe if I wasn't such a raging bitch of a teenager, then she wouldn't have gotten Alzheimer's. I had a long list of "if…then" scenarios in my mind. I always exchanged something for her Alzheimer's. I wasn't able to just accept it.

Next, there was depression. This stage of grief was definitely the most difficult and longest-lasting stage for me. It consumed my life for at least three years. Maybe more. I was in a deep, dark hole for so long. I never saw the light on the outside. I never thought I would get out of that damn hole. I was grieving and I never thought it would end. I couldn't find happiness in anything. If there ever was a smile on my face, it was probably forced. I was faking it. I was completely consumed with sadness, hopelessness, and despair. I cried *all* the time. I let the smallest things bother me and made them bigger than they should have been. Anything could set me off into a downward spiral. Nothing made me happy. I withdrew from the people and things that I loved. It was painful. Over time, I was eventually able to crawl out of that deep, dark hole. I still slip back into that hole sometimes, but I am able to crawl out of it much more quickly now. There are days that I feel sad and depressed, but it's not all day, every day. I no longer allow it to control my life.

The final stage of grief is acceptance. This is still something fairly new to me. For the first time, I can honestly say that I have accepted my mom's Alzheimer's. I'm doing all that I can do to help her fight it, to keep it from taking over her life and the lives of those who love her, and to raise Alzheimer's awareness. My acceptance is something that came with a great deal of time. Talking and writing about my mom's Alzheimer's were key in learning to accept it. I still have a hard time dealing with it sometimes, especially when new losses occur, but I have learned how to cope with it. I acknowledge that my mom has Alzheimer's and that it's only going to get worse. It sucks, but it is what it is.

When dealing with Alzheimer's, the grieving process is ongoing. It repeats itself over and over again. Just when you've come to accept a loss, you experience a new loss and the grieving process begins again. When a loved one has Alzheimer's, you lose a little bit more of that person each day. You are constantly losing, grieving, and accepting. Some losses hit you harder than others, but you are constantly repeating the stages of grief regardless of the significance of the loss. I'll talk more later about all that I've learned from my mom's Alzheimer's and what methods I use to cope with it.

So anyway, time flew by and before I knew it, it was September 2011, the week before our wedding. I had four nights of evening shift to get through before I would be off for almost three weeks. Steve was in training that week, so he was working during the day all week, while I worked at night. I went into work that first night with my final to-do list in hand. I have to admit, I don't think I did much work that night. I was in my patrol car, on my laptop, taking care of as much wedding business as I possibly could. We had to cross the final things off of our to-do list that week, in order to meet with our wedding coordinator later in the week to go over the final details. I had to finalize the seating chart. We had guests coming into town. We had to pack for our honeymoon. There was a lot left to do. All I was thinking about that night was our wedding.

It was about 11:00pm and I had just three more hours left of my shift. The squad that relieved us had already started their shift, so I was trying to lay low. I was sitting in a parking lot with a co-worker of mine. I was only half listening to the police radio as some of my fellow officers were getting dispatched to complaints. I remember hearing a few officers get dispatched to a disorderly conduct/theft from motor vehicle complaint in another district. Shortly after arriving on scene, Sergeant Joseph Szczerba got on the radio and asked for the suspect's description again. My co-worker and I made a joke about how Szczerba always found the suspect. He was like a god damned police K9. He sniffed them out. Then, Sgt. Szczerba said he was in foot pursuit of the suspect. We heard a struggle over the radio. Initially, it really wasn't anything unusual, but then the struggle continued for longer than it should have. My co-worker and I waited anxiously for Sgt. Szczerba to say that the suspect was in custody. But suddenly, Sgt. Szczerba asked for an ambulance and said, "I think I've been stabbed." He said it loudly, but calmly and clearly. It sounded like he had only been cut on the arm or something.

My co-worker and I hauled ass in our patrol vehicles to get to the scene, as I'm sure every other officer did at that time. We heard other officers saying on the radio that they had arrived on the scene. Then, one of the officers called on the radio for an officer down. I later found out that as those officers were arriving on the scene, Sgt. Szczerba collapsed right in front of them. Once I arrived on the scene, I saw Sgt. Szczerba being loaded into an ambulance as medical personnel were performing CPR on him. There was blood everywhere. That's all I saw. Blood. Was this real life? What the fuck was going on?

It was shortly after midnight when all of the officers on my squad were called to the hospital. We were told that Sergeant Joseph Szczerba had been pronounced dead. He fucking died. He had been stabbed to death. Murdered. Just like that. He was gone. We were all given a chance to go into the hospital room to say goodbye to Sgt. Szczerba. He looked like he was sleeping. Like he was going to wake up at any moment. I'll never forget it. It was so surreal.

Sgt. Szczerba was undoubtedly the best cop I had ever known. He cared more than anyone else. He was respected by every single person on our department and other departments, as well. He taught my class in the police academy and he was my field training supervisor. He was also my first supervisor when I was a rookie out on the street. I learned a lot from him, but probably still not as much as he wanted me to learn. He lived for police work and he loved every second of it. It was fun to him. He often said, "I would do this for free," and I believed it. The fact that he had just been stabbed to death was unimaginable.

I called Steve to tell him the horrific news and he immediately met us at the hospital. The members of my squad stayed at the hospital all night long until the medical examiner arrived to transport Sgt. Szczerba's body to their office for an autopsy. Officers lined the halls of the hospital and the sidewalk outside to salute Sgt. Szczerba as they brought his body out to the medical examiner's van. Tears ran continuously down my face. I don't think I stopped crying all night long. For once, I wasn't concerned about looking tough and strong. I wore my heart on my sleeve. I cried my eyes out. I gave myself a migraine. I felt sick. The whole night was a complete blur.

The next day was a blur, as well. By morning, all of the news programs were reporting that an officer from my police department had been stabbed to death. I had to call my parents to let them know that it wasn't me. I wished it was all a bad dream. I felt like a zombie. I didn't know what to do with myself. I tried to sleep, but that was impossible. I couldn't eat anything. I didn't know what to say to anyone. I had never experienced anything at all like this in my entire life. Everyone learned of the news and began to call or text me to find out what happened. I wanted to punch them all. I didn't want to talk to anyone about it.

My best friend at the time sent me a text message asking me if I was "friends" with the officer that was killed. I remember thinking, "What the fuck do you mean was I 'friends' with him?" No, I didn't consider us to be "friends." I was 26-years-old. He was married and in his forties. We didn't hang out after work or on our days off. We didn't call each other to chit chat. We had nothing in common other than where we worked. But, did any of that shit really matter?

He was my teacher, my leader, and my supervisor. I saw him every single day at work. More than I saw most of my friends and family. Aside from all of that, he was MURDERED. I wanted to ask my friend if she ever knew or worked with anyone that had been murdered. I wanted to ask her if she responded to the scene to assist. I wanted to ask her if she ever saw her co-worker's lifeless body being loaded into an ambulance. I wanted to ask her if she had ever seen that much blood. I got the feeling that she didn't think it was that big of a deal because I wasn't "friends" with the guy. Clearly, she didn't get it. No one did. The only people who understood were my fellow officers. At least we had each other.

We were given that night off, but returned to work the following night, only two nights after Sgt. Szczerba had been killed. I was barely holding myself together, but I had no choice. There was no way I was going to be the only one to stand up and say that I was having a hard time dealing with it. There were other officers who had been through much more than I had. Other officers had responded to the scene and witnessed Sgt. Szczerba collapse. They applied pressure to his wounds. They were covered in his blood. Other officers had known Sgt. Szczerba for a long time and were close friends of his. There was no way that I could show how I really felt. But, I was already an emotional wreck because of my mom and the fact that I was getting married in a week. Now this.

To top it all off, we realized that we wouldn't be able to attend Sgt. Szczerba's funeral. It was taking place on the day before our wedding. The same day as our wedding rehearsal and dinner. A police funeral is not just an hour or two long. A police funeral is an all-day event. There was no way that we would be able to attend. I was sick over it. I felt horrible about missing his funeral. I felt like I didn't deserve to be happy or excited about our wedding. I felt guilty if I allowed myself to think about anything other than his death. I felt empty. I felt like a zombie.

The night that Sgt. Szczerba was stabbed to death was the worst night of my life. The week after he was killed was the worst week of my life. I couldn't stop thinking about it. It was also the week before my wedding. It was supposed to be the best week of my life. I was overwhelmed and exhausted. I was spent. I was emotionally drained. My tears were all dried up. I felt nothing.

Somehow, I managed to drag myself through the next week. We managed to get everything crossed off of our wedding to-do list. We met with our wedding coordinator a few days before the wedding to go over the final details and to drop everything off at the venue. In the meantime, Sgt. Szczerba's wife had heard that we wouldn't be able to make it to his funeral because we were getting married the next day. She graciously invited us to the private family viewing so that we would have the opportunity to say our final goodbyes. The viewing was held on Thursday afternoon, two days before our wedding. It was surreal and emotional and about as bad as you would expect. We got through it and said our goodbyes, but I didn't feel any better.

Later that night, our out-of-town guests started to arrive. One of Steve's Army friends was coming over to our house for dinner. This was the first time I had ever met him. I couldn't even deal with any of it. I just wanted to hide under the covers in my bed. I had no choice but to continue on with all of our wedding plans that had been made long ago. The next day was Friday, the day of our rehearsal and rehearsal dinner, as well as the day of Sgt. Szczerba's funeral. I went to the nail salon with my mom and Melissa to get our pre-wedding manicures and pedicures. Not only was I feeling overwhelmed because it was the day before my wedding, but I also had to take care of my mom the whole time. Even though she had gotten a manicure every two weeks like clockwork for years, she no longer understood the process. She couldn't understand what the nail tech was asking her to do and she couldn't answer any of her questions. Melissa and I had to make sure that she was ok and try to include her in our conversation as best we could. As I was sitting there getting my manicure, I looked up at the TV screen and saw the news coverage of Sgt. Szczerba's funeral. I started crying in the middle of the nail salon. It was all just too much. I didn't know how I was going to get through the rest of the day, let alone the following day. My wedding day.

Finally, the big day had arrived. It was my wedding day. September 24, 2011. I was marrying my best friend and the person who knew me better than anyone else in the world. The man who just "got" me. I wanted to have the traditional night before my wedding where I spent the night at my parents' house. I didn't want to see Steve at all on our wedding day until the ceremony. This was something that I had always wanted. However, I struggled with my decision up until the end. Although it was what I had always wanted, I couldn't see myself spending the night at my parents' house, getting ready for my wedding there, and having professional wedding pictures taken there. My mom had always been a neat freak, who had kept her house immaculately clean and free of any clutter. Since she had been diagnosed with Alzheimer's, I hate to say it, but the house kind of turned to shit. It wasn't nearly as clean and organized as it had always been. It was dirty now. It was cluttered and messy. I just wasn't sure that I wanted to spend the night, take a shower, or get dressed in my wedding gown there. And, I was also a little embarrassed about the condition of their house. I was concerned about how the house was going to look as the background of my wedding photos. I had thought about just spending the night at my own house, but I really didn't want to see Steve on the morning of our wedding day. That meant that he would have to spend the night at a hotel, since he was from New Jersey and all of his family still lived there. I felt too guilty to make him do that. I went back and forth on my decision during the entire time we were planning our wedding.

In the end, I decided that I would spend the night and get ready at their house after all. I wanted to spare my mom and dad any hurt feelings about their own daughter not wanting to get ready at their house because she thought it was too dirty. My parents had cleaned up the house a little bit and my dad did an excellent job of making the backyard look beautiful for the background of my wedding pictures. So, my bridal party and I all got ready at my parents' house. We had our hair done, did our makeup, got dressed, and took pictures there. A limo picked us up to take us to the wedding venue, where we waited for the ceremony to begin. I remember being nervous that everything would go according to plan, as any bride would be, but I was also nervous about my mom's behavior and worried that she might do something to embarrass me. Looking back on it now, I feel incredibly selfish to have felt that way, but that's how I honestly felt. As it turned out, I had nothing to be worried about. Steve and I got married on a beautiful September day, outside on a covered patio, with a string quartet playing music throughout the ceremony. We had a very elegant, classy, black and white wedding reception. Absolutely everything went according to plan. Nothing went wrong. We had an absolutely perfect wedding.

Although many of the wedding details have escaped me by now, I do remember my mom on that day. She needed a lot of guidance and assistance while getting ready. I helped her get dressed and Melissa did her makeup. I had to constantly remind her of what she was supposed to do. It was more than her just being a nervous mother of the bride. In fact, I don't even think she realized that she was the mother of the bride. She didn't seem to have a clue as to what was going on that day. I ended up pulling our wedding coordinator aside at the venue to tell her that my mom had Alzheimer's. Our wedding coordinator was probably only the third person that I had ever told. I probably shouldn't have waited until the day of our wedding to tell her, but I did. I remember telling her to just kind of guide my mom in the right direction if she was wandering off or if she seemed confused. I was so worried about how my mom was going to eat, get a drink, or use the bathroom. But, I reminded myself that I was the bride and that it wasn't my responsibility to help her that day. Someone else would have to take care of her. Today was *my* day.

I saw the look of confusion on my mom's face when she saw various family members that she had not seen in a while. She didn't remember who they were or how they were related to us. She looked like a lost little girl, dancing the night away on the edge of the dance floor, all by herself. I saw as my dad and other family members tried to convince her to take a break or have a drink of water. She refused and just brushed them off, like a little girl refusing a nap. She just wanted to dance. On one hand, I was so glad to see her having fun. She didn't have a care in the world. She embodied the expression "dance like no one is watching." But, on the other hand, it saddened me to see her so lost, alone, and withdrawn. I was also a little embarrassed by her dancing. It was as if there was no one else in the room. She wasn't socializing with anyone. I remember going up to her to dance at one point and being disgusted because she was so sweaty from dancing all night. I didn't really want to touch her so I was trying to keep my distance from her while we were dancing. I think we only danced for one song. It could have been a memorable moment, but I fucking ruined it by being so selfish. The photographer snapped a picture of us dancing and I have this disgusted look on my face. I hate that fucking picture. I cringe every time I look at it.

I felt like all of the big moments of the night were completely lost on my mom. She didn't understand what was going on that night. She didn't play the role of the mother of the bride. She reminded me so much of a little girl. A lost child. She was in her own little bubble that night. I guess I should have been grateful though. I've seen how mothers of the bride can ruin an entire wedding by being an extreme, stuck up, pain in the ass. At least I didn't have that problem. But, I wasn't thinking about that at the time. I was just sad. I felt like my mom's body had been at my wedding, but her mind was somewhere else entirely.

The other big thing that I remember about my wedding day was that I didn't cry at all. Not once. Not even one single tear. I think I was too emotionally drained that day to cry. I had cried so much in the months, weeks, and days leading up to my wedding day that I couldn't even muster up one lousy tear. Meanwhile, Steve blubbered his way through our wedding vows. He cried like a baby. He was so emotional during the ceremony. I was honestly pretty surprised. I thought for sure that I would've been the one crying like a baby. I had said it all along. I couldn't believe it when I heard his voice crack after saying the first few words of our vows. In that moment, I definitely fell in love with him a little bit more. I knew how much he loved me and cared about me. I knew that he would always truly be there for me, through thick and thin. I knew that he would be the only person who could help me through the tough days that would come with my mom's Alzheimer's. He might not always be able to understand exactly what I was going through, but I knew that he would always care and be there to support me.

Our honeymoon couldn't have come at a better time. I think I was actually more excited for the honeymoon than I was for the wedding itself. It was the perfect time for us to get away from everything and just relax. It was the perfect time to get away from all of the family and friends that we had been spending way too much time with. It was also the perfect time to get away from work and all of the sadness and suffering following the difficult loss of Sgt. Szczerba. I couldn't have been happier to get away from it all. To relax and refresh. We spent a week in Aruba. It was beautiful. I only turned my cell phone on two or three times to call home. I was completely disconnected from my real life and all of the problems I had left back home. It was glorious. At the end of the week, I felt ready to return home and get back to some sense of normalcy. I was ready to get back to reality and to develop a more positive attitude. I wanted to try to embrace a new outlook on life. I just wanted to find a way to be happy again.

It's Time for a Change

I returned to work with a more positive attitude after my wedding. I thought that maybe if I just went into work each day with a smile on my face, then I would be happier working there. I decided to just try to do my job the best that I could and go home to my new husband every night. I would try harder to enjoy my days off and make more of an effort to see my mom. I thought this whole positive outlook thing might actually work. It didn't. After a few weeks, I was still as miserable as could be with my job. I was tired of working crazy hours and never having off when my friends and family had off. I was tired of missing out on weekends, holidays, and family parties. I was tired of dealing with other people's shit. Both the people that I dealt with on the street and the people that I dealt with on the department.

For the most part, I liked the people that I worked *with*, but I didn't like the people that I worked *for*. I was always worried about what dumb shit they were going to get on me for next. It was never anything important. I never caused any problems at work and I had never been disciplined for anything. Not even once. Still, some supervisor was always getting on me about something completely petty and ridiculous. Some stupid administrative thing. "Why didn't you do this?" "Why was this form late?" "Why did you let that complaint pend for so long?" "Why didn't you call that person back sooner?" "Why don't you make more car stops?" "Why did you make that car stop? Were you trying to get out of handling a complaint?" I knew how to do my job and I felt that I did it well. I was capable of making good decisions, writing good reports, and my supervisors never had to worry about me out on the street. I was capable of handling anything that came my way. I always answered up on the radio to respond to complaints and to assist other officers. However, it was never about what I was doing right. It was always about what I was doing wrong. No matter how much work I did, I was always being treated like I was lazy for what I didn't do. They always acted like everyone was trying to get out of doing work. I just couldn't deal with it anymore. I was also tired of arguing with everyone that I came into contact with. I was tired of having to prove myself as a young female police officer, day in and day out. Don't get me wrong. I *could* handle it. I just didn't *want* to anymore. I fucking hated dealing with people. I avoided them at all costs. And, I was tired of not having a regular sleep cycle. I hated going into work late at night and going to bed in the morning. I hated waking up every day feeling like I had a hangover when I didn't even drink. I started looking for a new job and applying to positions in other fields. As soon as I found another job, I was going to get the hell out of there.

Meanwhile, I was doing the best I could with my mom. I would make an effort to call her at least once during my work week. But, that was often easier said than done. Sometimes, the only time I had a chance to call her was while I was at work. It was difficult to try to have a conversation with her, while also listening to the police radio, driving, or paying attention to whatever else I was doing. I could barely have a conversation with her without any distractions, let alone trying to balance all of these things at once. If I got dispatched to a complaint while I was on the phone with her, it would take at least a few minutes to try to get off the phone with her. She just kept on talking. She didn't understand that I had to go, like, right now. And, police officers don't get a lunch or dinner break, so it wasn't like I could just call her during that time. It was easier if I could just call her during my time off. However, I had limited time off between shifts. I was either eating, sleeping, working out, making dinner, or getting ready for my next shift. I never had more than five minutes to spare. Many times, my work week would go by and I would realize that I hadn't talked to my mom in four or five days. Normally, that wouldn't seem like a big deal, but, given the fact that she had Alzheimer's, it was a big deal to me. I always felt so horribly guilty that I hadn't talked to her in so long. I would try to make up for it on my days off, but I never had anything to talk to her about. She didn't really understand my job or the stories I would tell her. I also didn't want to tell her too many stories because I didn't want to upset or worry her. Immediately after I hung up the phone with her, I would always look at the duration of our phone call. It was like I wanted to make sure that I had talked to her for long enough. If the conversation was short, I felt the need to justify it to myself. No matter how often I called her or how long we spoke, it was never enough. I was always left feeling empty and guilty.

Aside from calling her, I would try to stop by my mom's house to see her at least once during my days off. It was usually only for an hour or so on my way home from the gym, but I did what I could. It became increasingly hard and depressing to go to my parents' house. I felt like everything was going to shit. Due to my mom's Alzheimer's, her ability to keep a clean house had greatly diminished. My mom's house had always been very well kept. There was never any clutter in sight. Everything was always nice and clean. Her house was immaculate.

Now, it seemed as though every surface in the house was covered with crap. There were things strewn about all over the place. Items were in places that it didn't even make sense for them to be. The bread box was full of note pads, pens, and paper. The utensils were distributed unevenly between two or three different drawers and cabinets. Random items were piled up in each of the bedrooms, so much so that it was impossible to even walk into these rooms. My parents' bedroom had a lot of clutter, as well. Mismatched shoes were in boxes on the floor. There were piles of clothes on the floor. There was an old comforter and decorative pillows in the corner. My parents' clothes were randomly scattered among the four bedrooms upstairs. My mom's clothes were in my dad's dresser drawers and vice versa. The dishes in the kitchen were never cleaned well enough. The bathrooms were disgusting and dirty, with soap scum, mildew, and dust bunnies everywhere. Their house had never looked this way when I was growing up there. It was very difficult for me to see it this way. My mom had not only lost the ability to physically clean, but she couldn't remember how to do it anymore. She never knew what to do or what products to use to clean a certain room. It seemed as if she didn't even remember that she was supposed to clean the house. It was like the thought to clean had never even occurred to her.

My parents always had a very traditional marriage. My dad worked full-time, while my mom was a full-time housewife and stay-at-home mom. She took care of all of the cleaning, laundry, cooking, paying the bills, grocery shopping, etc. Once she stopped doing these things, they simply weren't getting done. After a while, my dad had no choice but to take over. Not only was he already working a full-time job, but now he was also taking care of all of the household chores that my mom had always done. I don't remember ever seeing my dad do a load of laundry, vacuum, or mop the floors. Not ever in my whole entire life. Not until my mom got Alzheimer's. These tasks were all new to him and it was a lot for him to keep up with. Therefore, whenever I went over to their house, it appeared as though it had not been cleaned in months or more. It probably hadn't been cleaned in that long. I always felt so bad that my dad didn't have anyone to help around the house. My dad was never the type of person to ask for help. He always tried to handle everything by himself. At the time, I honestly don't think it ever even occurred to me to offer to help him. I was too busy and too wrapped up in my own life. I never really thought about it until I stepped foot inside of their house. And even then, I tried to forget about it as soon as I left.

The other reason I hated going to my parents' house was that I would always notice that my mom's condition seemed to be getting much worse. At the time, my dad was still going to work every day and leaving my mom at home alone. I would usually go over to visit her in the middle of the day, on a weekday, while my dad was still at work. More often than not, she was still in her pajamas and a bathrobe when I arrived. I don't think it ever occurred to her to get dressed. Sure, she had nowhere to go and no one to impress, but my mom had always gotten dressed, did her hair, and put on some makeup, even just to sit around her house all day. So, to see my mom in her pajamas all day, with greasy, unwashed hair and no makeup on, was upsetting to me. I'm not sure if it was that she had forgotten how to get dressed and ready for the day, or if she just forgot that she was supposed to get dressed each day. I think that maybe she had forgotten how to get dressed so trying to do so just overwhelmed her and stressed her out. Therefore, she just tried to avoid the entire process whenever possible. Either way, it made me feel sad and depressed to see her that way. It also upset me that most of the times I went over to her house, she was half asleep in her chair in the family room. The TV was always on, but I know that she had no clue what she was watching. I would always try to convince her to go outside and sit on the porch or take a walk, but she never would. I wasn't even completely confident that if she did take a walk by herself, she would remember how to get back to her house. Her condition was becoming increasingly worse and it was hard to watch.

We were kind of in limbo at that time. My mom's condition was not yet so bad that she couldn't be left home alone for a while, but it was bad enough that she couldn't really take care of herself either. I worried about her all the time. I worried that something might happen to her while she was home alone. What if she had a medical emergency and didn't know how to dial 9-1-1? What if a stranger knocked on the door and she let him come inside? I was a cop. I knew that there were all kinds of crazy assholes out there just waiting for the opportunity to take advantage of someone like my mom. What if she turned on the stovetop, forgot about it, and started a fire? Although, my mom never liked to cook anyway so that scenario was a little less likely, but still possible. All kinds of scenarios would run through my mind and I was in a constant state of panic as to what might happen to her. Any time my mom called me, I answered immediately, no matter what I was doing. I was always afraid that she was going to call me because she really needed me and I didn't want to think about what might happen if I didn't answer the phone. Even if she called me while I was sleeping during the day after working the midnight shift, I always answered the phone. I was too afraid not to. I had my phone with me at all times. It was always on and the ringer volume was always turned all the way up.

On top of everything else, my parents' dog, a black lab named Dakota, was getting old and not doing very well. I think he was about thirteen or fourteen years old at the time. Dakota was the sweetest, most lovable dog in the world. He had been a member of our family since I was about thirteen years old. My dad loved that dog more than anything else. They were best pals. My dad would take him to several different parks on the weekends to go for walks. He still took Dakota to these parks when Dakota wasn't even able to walk around anymore. My dad would have done anything for that dog. Anything to make him live forever. Being that we're a huge dog-loving family, we've always treated every dog we've owned as part of the family. Dakota was different. He was my dad's companion. His buddy. His stress relief. Dakota was home all day with my mom when no one else was around. However, like any other dog, Dakota started to deteriorate with age. At first, he was having trouble walking and getting up the stairs. Then, he was having trouble even standing up at all. It got so bad that Dakota was no longer able to control his bladder or bowel movements. I feel terrible saying this, but Dakota should've been put out of his misery long before he finally was. My dad had such a bond with Dakota and the situation with my mom only made it that much more difficult for him to let go.

I hated going over to their house and seeing Dakota the way he was. He had been my childhood pet. And now, he would just lay around all day, whining and barking. I believe it was because he was in constant pain and misery. I believe that he was suffering due to his old age. Dakota would have accidents all day long. He would pee while lying on the floor or on his bed. He would pee as soon as you stood him up. Dakota would also poop while lying down or while walking. There were many times when I went over to my parents' house and smelled the poop as soon as I opened the door. It smelled so bad that I would gag. My mom never even noticed when Dakota had pooped in the house. He would lay there in his own shit for hours because my mom didn't realize what had happened. Sometimes, she did notice that he had an accident so she would make an attempt to clean it up. However, she was never able to clean it all up and there was always some left behind. I would walk around their house and see poop smeared along the walls or baseboards. The floors and carpets were never completely cleaned up and there were stains everywhere. Many times, I would walk into their house to see a pile of poop lying somewhere on the floor. Dakota always had poop smeared on his butt or remnants in his fur.

I know it sounds completely disgusting and gross, but my mom was just incapable of noticing any of this or cleaning it up. I always felt that it was completely unfair to my mom to be left in this situation to care for Dakota while my dad was at work. My mom didn't even know how to take care of herself anymore. How could she be expected to take care of a dog? Still, I completely understood the love my dad had for Dakota and why it was so difficult for him to let go. It might not seem like that big of a deal, but it was a very difficult and delicate situation for our family. And, my dad had made up his mind that he did not want to put Dakota down. He just wanted Dakota to die on his own, so he waited.

All of these factors combined made me feel incredibly guilty for not being around to help my family out more. While all of these problems were going on with my own family, I was helping other people and their families solve their problems. Most of the time, I felt like their problems weren't even real problems to begin with. I was stuck working at a job that I absolutely hated. I was still searching for new jobs and applying to anything that seemed even remotely interesting to me. I would spend all of my down time at work looking for a new job. I was applying for jobs on my laptop, in my patrol car, while I was at work. I was desperate to get the hell out of there. It made no sense for me to continue working at a job that made me so miserable. It made no sense that this job took away from me being able to help my family and spend time with my mom. I dreaded going to work every day. Often times, my days off were spent being miserable, irritable, and dreading the thought of having to go back to work. It was consuming my life. I really wanted to do the responsible thing and find a new job before I left my current one. It just seemed hopeless to me. I had applied for countless jobs in other fields, but, since I didn't have the required education or experience in those fields, I wasn't having any luck. It was so frustrating.

At the end of March 2013, I decided to say fuck being responsible. I went into work one evening and was told that I was being assigned to work in a different district. I was told that it was because I had done something to upset the chief of our department. Come the fuck on! What the hell could I have possibly done? I was pretty sure that the chief didn't even know my name or that I existed. In my mind, that was a *good* thing! It meant that all I ever did was show up to work, keep my head down and my mouth shut, and do my job. I decided that I needed to stick up for myself for once and ask what exactly I had done wrong. I was told that when the chief came into the roll call room to talk to my squad one morning before our shift, I appeared to be "disinterested" in what he had to say. Apparently, this offended him a great deal. When I asked if I had done something specifically to appear "disinterested," I was told that it was just my "general demeanor and appearance." Really?! So, let me get this straight. He was offended by my general demeanor and appearance? What the fuck? I guess I should have been sitting on the edge of my seat, drooling over his every word.

I was also told that my "disinterest" during the chief's speech prompted him to "look into" me. What he discovered was that my statistical monthly average was consistently lower than what he deemed acceptable. Basically, this meant that I wasn't conducting enough vehicle stops or issuing enough traffic citations to please him. My reason was that there were never enough officers working in my area to provide back up if something went wrong during one of these vehicle stops. I felt as though it was completely unsafe for anyone to conduct proactive policing (vehicle or pedestrian stops) when there weren't enough officers working in the area. This had been my argument consistently for the last five years, but nothing had ever changed. The chief disagreed and he didn't care. His priority seemed to be focused on stats rather than officer safety. He wanted something to be done about my "low stats", so the lieutenant of my squad assigned me to work in a different district. It was what I considered "unofficial discipline" for my actions. Put bluntly, it was a punishment meant to motivate me to stop more cars. Their priorities were too screwed up to realize that my low statistical monthly average was due to horrific staffing, and certainly not laziness on my part. I was furious.

I realized that I was quickly going to become a target. I was on the chief's radar now. He was going to find any reason to discipline me for something, anything. All because I wasn't willing to stroke anyone's ego or kiss anyone's ass. Haven't they ever heard of a resting bitch face? Maybe I was disinterested in what he had to say. Or, maybe I was thinking about all of the other shit that I had going on in my life. Maybe I was thinking about how I never had time to go to my parents' house and, when I did, I never knew what the hell I'd be walking into. No one ever bothered to ask me. They just judged me by my demeanor and appearance, looked into me, and decided to punish me by moving me to another district. It was bullshit! I had never received official discipline for anything. Not once in the five years that I had worked there. However, I was constantly made to feel worthless and lazy because of my low stats. Those exact words were often used to describe officers with low stats. I was a good officer and a valuable asset to the police department in many other areas. Areas where plenty of other officers were significantly lacking. But, none of that mattered because I had low stats. I was fucking tired of it.

Steve and I discussed everything at length. I went home "sick" that night so I could write my resignation letter. Enough was enough and I was completely over it. It was time to move on. Even though I didn't have another job lined up, I didn't care. I decided that I would take some time off and help out with my mom. I knew that everything would work out and that I would eventually find another job. I just had to look out for myself and do what was best for me. I submitted my resignation letter on April Fools' Day 2013. It felt absolutely amazing. And also, fitting, since I always thought that working there was a joke. It was honestly one of the best days of my life. I had often dreamt about what it would be like to not be a cop anymore. I hated the hours. I hated the people. I hated the bullshit. I hated dealing with other people's often insignificant problems when I had actual problems of my own to deal with. I hated constantly having someone breathing down my neck, telling me how to do my job, micromanaging me. I hated that no one ever trusted me. I hated never being right and always being wrong. I hated that I had become a miserable, irritable, anti-social bitch. I had never liked people all that much to begin with, but now, I pretty much hated everyone. I wanted nothing to do with all of the dumb-ass people that I had been dealing with day in and day out. I was beyond excited to let all of that shit go. I was ready to start my new life as a *normal* person.

Becoming a Caregiver

After talking to my dad about my decision to quit the police department, he agreed that I had done the right thing. I think he was a little disappointed that his little girl wasn't going to be a badass cop anymore, but he completely understood why I wanted to resign. He offered to pay me to help take care of my mom and clean their house, until I figured out what I wanted to do next. I agreed. It would allow me to spend more time with my mom and I would be making a little bit of money, too. And, I didn't feel bad about my dad paying me because I knew it was going to be a lot of work. Looking back now, I wish I had taken at least a few days off after quitting my job to just sit around and do absolutely nothing. Instead, I got right to work helping my parents. The first day that my husband left for work without me, I went straight to my parents' house and started "working" for my dad. I think I just felt so guilty and lazy for quitting my job without having another job lined up that I wanted to feel like I was contributing in some way.

My first assignment was to declutter my parents' house. So, I started cleaning up and decluttering their house right away. It was quite a task because almost every surface was covered with stuff. All of the bedrooms were full of stuff. The closets were full. The drawers were full. The floors were covered with all kinds of stuff. I started going through everything, deciding what to keep and what to donate. I threw a lot of stuff away. I had garbage bags upon garbage bags full of stuff that I had decided they did not need. I cleaned each room and organized the items that I had decided to keep. I started to make sense of each room. Little by little, I was clearing out closets, drawers, and floor space. The pile of donations was growing and growing. I felt like I was getting somewhere and I was proud of what I had already accomplished in a short time.

I remember that I started to feel frustrated when I would go to my parents' house and see that my work was becoming undone. The closets and spaces that I had spent hours clearing out were filling up again. I felt like I was starting over each and every time I went to their house. For example, I had organized my mom's clothes in her closet. I had to split her clothes into two separate closets because she had so much stuff. The clothes that were appropriate for the current season went into the master bedroom closet. The clothes that were not in season went into a spare bedroom closet. I was starting to notice that my mom had been going through her clothes and moving stuff around. She was mixing up the clothes for different seasons. She was taking stuff off of the hangers and not putting it back properly, if at all. I had paired each of her shoes with its match and put them away in her shoe boxes. My mom had gone through her shoes and made a mess of them. There were boxes and boxes of mismatched shoes. Some boxes contained only one shoe, while other boxes contained three shoes. And, don't even get me started on her dresser drawers. She had made an even bigger mess of them.

I mean, who can blame a girl for wanting to play with and try on her clothes and shoes, but I was so frustrated. My mom no longer understood how to put things away properly or where to put them. She would take something out to look at it or try it on and she would put it back in some random place. Everything was getting all mixed up again. My mom even went through my dad's stuff and mixed it all up with her stuff. She took things that belonged to him and put them in her dresser drawers or her closet. Because of this, I actually ended up throwing away a gold watch that my dad had received when he retired from his electrical union. It was in one of my mom's drawers with a bunch of junk jewelry, so I just threw it away with the pile, thinking it was nothing. I felt terrible when my dad asked me if I had seen the watch and I realized what I had done. What was the point in me doing all of this work if my mom was going to undo it all? The best part was that she denied doing any of it. She would say that she hadn't been in that closet or that drawer. She said that she didn't touch anything or move it from its place. She could never tell me who had made the mess, but she always said that it wasn't her. It didn't even matter where either one of us put anything anyway. No matter where everything was, she still had no idea where to find anything.

I should probably also mention that I have major obsessive compulsive disorder, or OCD. It drives me absolutely nuts when things are out of their place. I always feel the need to straighten things up and put them away "just so." I probably spend at least an hour a day straightening up my own house, which is already obsessively neat and organized to begin with. It takes me an hour to fold and put away one load of laundry. It takes me at least a half an hour to unload the dishwasher and put the dishes away. I admittedly can't stand having people over my house because it gives me a great deal of anxiety when anyone touches or moves my stuff around. I constantly follow my husband around and "fix" what he has just put away.

Needless to say, being in a constant state of disorganization at my parents' house was taking a major toll on my OCD. I would spend hours a day organizing different rooms in their house only for it to be undone by the next day. Every time I went over there, I would check on the work I had done the previous day. If I found even one thing out of place, I would freak out and organize it to absolute perfection once again. I literally cringed every time I walked into their house and saw the mess that was waiting for me to clean up. I didn't understand how they could stand to live in such a messy house. It made me anxious just being there for five minutes. I would go home and take it out on my own house, spending even more time straightening it up. I was in a constant state of anxiety. I was driving myself crazy.

Aside from clearing out and organizing the house, my dad would ask me to help with other things. Sometimes, he had laundry for me to do or a room that needed to be cleaned. He had me run almost all of their dishes through the dishwasher because my mom hadn't been cleaning them well enough by hand. He actually didn't even know that they had a dishwasher. I had to show him how to use the dishwasher because he had never done it before. I remember my mom was also surprised to find out that they had a dishwasher. She claimed that she never knew they had one, even though she used to use it all the time. Sometimes, my dad would have me run errands for him. I also got into the habit of taking my mom to our hairdresser for her hair appointments. It was actually a pretty good deal for me since my dad would pay for me to get my hair done, as well.

One day, my mom and I painstakingly went through every item of clothing in her closet to see what fit and what didn't. I basically had to put the clothes on my mom for her because she had such a hard time getting dressed. At the time, I had very little patience with her and it was just easier if I did it myself, rather than waiting for her to figure it out. Then, my dad had me take my mom shopping for some things that she needed. She practically got a whole new wardrobe. We spent hours at the store because my mom had no idea what size she wore and she had to try on absolutely everything. I remember standing in the fitting room with her while I put the clothes on her and took them off again. She looked so small and frail, so lost and confused. Here I was dressing my mom. It broke my heart. How did we get here?

Once we got home, I put away her new clothes and organized all of her clothes by season again. I took all of the clothes we were donating to Goodwill, along with a bunch of other donated items. I'll never forget when she called me the next day because she had gotten lost in her own closet. She had gone into her master bedroom closet to look for her new clothes and she couldn't figure out how to get out. Once she got out of the closet, she couldn't figure out how to get out of her bedroom and downstairs to the living room. I was able to talk her through it without having to go over to her house, but I was very worried that she was now becoming disoriented in her own home. What made it even worse was that she was clearly embarrassed by her mistake and kept saying that she was stupid. I assured her that she was not stupid, but I couldn't hide the fact that my heart was breaking.

After a couple of months at my new job, I was already stressed out and overwhelmed. It was very difficult for me to be around my mom so much and to see her constantly declining. I became the go-to person for everything. Any time my mom or dad needed help with anything, it was on me to help them out. I wasn't working anymore and I only lived about two miles away from them. Don't get me wrong. I loved being able to help them out so much, but it was overwhelming at times. It became expected of me. I ended up going over to their house almost every day of the week, even on days that I had not planned on going over there. Sometimes, I needed a break for a day or two, so I would tell my dad that I couldn't come over that day. On those days, I would still call my mom once or twice to check in on her while my dad was at work.

I remember calling her to check in on her and sometimes she would answer the phone in a panic because she had gotten lost in her house again. She was looking for the bathroom or the kitchen and she couldn't find it. She always seemed hesitant to tell me what was going on because she was embarrassed by her mistake. One time, I called to check on her and she said that she couldn't figure out how to turn on the television. I knew that there was no way I could explain it to her over the phone. I also knew that she really had nothing else to do all day while my dad was at work, except watch TV. I offered to come over to turn it on for her, but she said that I didn't have to do that. The thought of her sitting and staring at the wall all day just about killed me, so I ended up driving over to her house just to turn on the TV. Another time, my Nan (my mom's mom) called me because she had tried to call my mom, but didn't get an answer. She talked to my mom every morning and she was very worried that she couldn't get a hold of her. I tried calling her myself with no answer and was about to get in my car to drive over there when I finally got a hold of her. Do you see a pattern here? I felt like I was driving over to my parents' house every five minutes for one reason or another. And, these were the days that I was supposed to have "off."

The days that I did go to my parents' house to help out were becoming increasingly more difficult, as well. It was almost impossible for me to get anything done while I was there. My parents' dog, Dakota, was only getting worse. It seemed like I ended up spending more time taking care of him than doing anything else. Poor Dakota was unable to stand up on his own anymore. He would just lay there, whining and barking, until someone helped him stand up. Once I got him standing up, he would just pee all over me, himself, and the floor. I would have to stop what I was doing to clean up the mess and get him settled in again. He would still just lay there, whining and barking, all day long. There was nothing that I could do to help him or make him feel better.

I always felt really bad for my mom because she would get so upset when this happened. She didn't know how to take care of Dakota anymore and it really upset her to see him like that. My dad called the vet almost every day it seemed to see what they could do for Dakota. There really wasn't anything that anyone could do. My dad had made it clear to everyone that he never wanted to put Dakota down. I think he kept calling the vet every day because he was hoping that there would be some new magic answer. I just kept thinking that Dakota had had enough and that it was unfair to him to continue living this way. My dad would text me all the time and say that he was thinking about taking Dakota to the vet to be put down, that it was time to do something. But, by the time I got to his house, he had already changed his mind and wasn't going to do anything yet. He would say, "See? Look, look. He's doing so much better now." I understood that my dad was very reluctant to let go of his best bud and that he didn't want to have to make that decision. I understood that he was also concerned about how it would affect my mom. He just kept waiting for Dakota to die on his own, but it seemed like that was never going to happen. It was so frustrating.

It was very hard for me to see Dakota in that condition, just laying around, waiting to die. I am a big animal lover and I am completely obsessed with dogs. I considered Dakota to be my brother. I didn't know how much longer I could stand to look at him like that. I decided to work on convincing my dad that it was time to let Dakota go. I talked to my dad about it as often as I could. Eventually, I convinced him that it was the right thing to do. One day, Dakota was having a really bad day and my dad had to come home from work. He had talked to the vet, who said that my dad could bring Dakota in during her lunch break to have him put down. It took all I had to convince my dad to go through with it. I had to keep telling him that it was the right thing to do, all the way to the vet's office. I felt like the biggest asshole in the entire world, but I knew it really was the right thing to do.

My sister stayed back at the house with my mom, since we had all decided that it would be best for my mom not to be there. I was completely shocked that my dad actually followed through with it and Dakota was put to sleep that day. The vet and her vet tech had become very familiar with my dad, my mom, and Dakota. They knew and understood that it was a very tough decision and a very delicate situation. I am still grateful to this day for the way the vet and her vet tech handled everything. They didn't rush it. They let us say our goodbyes to Dakota. They were very kind, gentle, and reassuring through it all. There was not a dry eye in that room when Dakota took his last breath.

We left the vet's office with Dakota's body, which was all wrapped up and ready to be buried. We went back to my parent's house and prepared to bury Dakota in the backyard. My dad had already dug a hole in the ground weeks before, knowing that he would need it soon. We placed Dakota's body into a box and placed the box into the hole. I helped my dad shovel dirt on top of the box until it was completely buried. This would have been a difficult situation for any family to go through. No one wanted to have to make the decision to put a dog down and then have to bury him/her in the backyard. It would have been hard for any family to say goodbye to a beloved pet. But, I cannot describe the pain, hurt, and sadness that I felt that day, helping my dad bury our family dog. It was so much more than that to us.

My dad had lost his companion, his buddy, his solace. I knew that he felt alone now. There would be no one there to comfort him when he was having a rough time with my mom. I also knew that my dad felt incredibly guilty for making the decision to put Dakota down. He felt like it wasn't his place to decide when it was time for Dakota to die. My mom actually seemed to handle it pretty well, but, then again, I think that was mostly because she didn't really understand what was going on. I knew that she was sad that Dakota was gone and that she would never see him again, but I think she was also a little bit relieved that she didn't have to try to take care of him anymore. In some ways, I feel like Dakota's death made us all realize the sadness of our reality. There was no longer anything to distract us from my mom's Alzheimer's. There was no longer a sick dog to focus on or take care of. It was time for us to focus on my mom and to take care of her. It was time for us to face reality.

Shit's Getting Real

Now that Dakota was no longer with us, I was able to focus on taking care of my mom when I went to her house. When he was still living, I was never able to get my mom out of the house and take her places. I was constantly worried about leaving Dakota home alone. I was afraid that he would just be laying there in his own pee and poop, whining and suffering, with no one to help him get up. I wouldn't dare leave him home alone in order to take my mom out somewhere. It often felt like we were both prisoners in my parents' house. It might sound a bit harsh, but once Dakota was put out of his misery, it was a huge relief for me. I felt like I was finally able to really take care of my mom and take her out so that she wasn't just sitting at home in front of the television all the time. We were finally free to go and do things, get out in the fresh air, and get away from that damn house. We were no longer stuck inside.

We didn't go out every single time that I went over to my mom's house and we never went anywhere far. We would usually just go out to lunch or go shopping. My mom had a slight obsession with Boscov's at the time and we would often go there. Sometimes we went shopping for me, too. On a few occasions, we drove up to my Aunt Diane's house to visit with her and Nan, my grandmother. On most days, we would just go to the park to take my dog, Oakley, for a walk. Our two favorite parks were Glasgow Park and Battery Park, which is in Old New Castle, by the Delaware River. My mom loved to just sit there on a park bench for hours, watching the boats go by and listening to the water and the geese. Oakley reminded my mom a lot of Dakota, as they were both male black labs. She loved spending time with him and being able to take him for walks with me. Oakley is the sweetest, gentlest, and most loving dog you could ever meet. He made for an excellent therapy dog for my mom. I could just see the happiness, calmness, and peacefulness in her eyes when she was with Oakley.

When Dakota was still living, I was very hesitant to bring Oakley with me to my mom's house. At the time, he was only about three years old and he still had the energy of a puppy. Anyone who knows Labradors knows that they don't start to calm down until they're about five years old. I was very nervous that Oakley would be too wild and crazy around Dakota and that he might hurt him.

Therefore, most of the time, I didn't bring Oakley with me when I went to my parents' house to help out. I only brought him when my dad was home and he wanted to see Oakley. Once Dakota was no longer a concern, I started bringing Oakley with me every time I went. I saw my mom light up around him. I knew how useful she felt when I would ask her to watch Oakley for me while I did something upstairs. I saw how proud she was when I let her hold the leash while we took Oakley for a walk. I would say that Oakley is part human, but he is really so much more than that. I can't even put into words how special Oakley is to me. He is my baby boy. He's got a heart and soul like no human being I've ever met. He brought my mom to life. And, he was there to comfort me on the tough days. He was my loyal and understanding companion. He always knew what to do and what we needed. He just knew.

Here's just one example. On the day that my dad and I took Dakota to the vet to be put down, I had left Oakley at home. Once we got back to my parents' house and buried Dakota in the backyard, my husband called me to say that he was home from work. I asked him to come over and to bring Oakley with him. I figured that Oakley might be able to relieve some of the stress, tension, and sadness that we were all feeling. So, my husband brought Oakley over and he ran all around their backyard like he usually did. Suddenly, I looked over at Dakota's grave and noticed that Oakley had plopped down right on top of it. My first instinct was to yell at him to move and to get off of the grave. But then, I realized that Oakley was sitting there for a reason. He knew that Dakota was there

70

and he was trying to comfort his old pal. He just laid there until he was ready to get up. Of all the places in that backyard for him to lay down, he chose the exact spot where Dakota was buried. He had to know. When Oakley, my husband, and I all went home, I went straight upstairs to our bedroom to lay down and cry for a while. I was emotionally drained and overwhelmed from the day's events. Oakley came up to the bedroom with me and laid right there next to me until I was done crying. He stayed by my side the whole time and comforted me. Like I said before, he just knew what he was supposed to do.

I continued to take Oakley with me every time I went over to my mom's house. Oakley even stayed with them for a week while my husband and I went to Denver for a vacation. My mom loved having Oakley there so much that she didn't want to give him back. Of course, I would never let that happen. Oakley would hang out with my mom and play outside, while I cleaned, did laundry, and continued to try to organize the house. Along with enjoying Oakley's company and discovering the outdoors again, my mom also discovered that they owned a cat, Ravyn. Now, just because my mom had just discovered Ravyn, it doesn't mean that they had just gotten her. I had actually brought Ravyn home as a stray when I was about 16 years old. My mom had just forgotten about her over the years. Let me tell you why.

When my mom first started displaying the signs and symptoms of Alzheimer's, one thing that we noticed was that she had become obsessed with their cat. She was terrified that Ravyn, who was strictly an indoor cat, was going to get out of the house somehow. Whenever anyone opened the door to enter or exit the house, she would run around the house, frantically looking for Ravyn to make sure that she hadn't gotten out. We all used to make fun of her and mock her for doing that. Of course, that was before we knew any better. My mom became so consumed with the thought of losing Ravyn that she began to keep her locked away in my sister's old bedroom, with the door closed, at all times. She would even write these barely legible signs to hang on the bedroom door, warning people that there was a cat inside and not to let her out of the room. This went on for years. After keeping Ravyn shut up in that room for so long, I guess my mom had just forgotten all about her.

I've said before that I'm a huge animal lover and I would never want to see an animal being neglected. I often felt guilty that I allowed for Ravyn to be locked up in that bedroom for so long. My only excuse was that I had a lot of other shit to worry about at the time. Dakota was still living and he needed a lot of care. Ravyn had shelter, food, water, and a litter box. She wasn't being abused, but I did feel that she had been neglected for a long time. She became afraid of people and other animals because she was never allowed out of that bedroom. In my defense, it was easier to just keep Ravyn in that room than it was to deal with my mom freaking out over Ravyn being let out. I would always go into her room to check on her when I went over to my mom's house. Oakley would sit outside of the bedroom door, whining. He desperately wanted to meet Ravyn and become her friend. He knew that she was in that room and he wanted to get in there so badly. I just didn't want to deal with the consequences of letting Ravyn out of the room.

One of the first things that I did after Dakota passed away was open that bedroom door and let Ravyn out. At first, she didn't even want to come out of the room. She would sit in there on the bed and meow constantly. Eventually, she came out into the hallway and slowly, over a long period of time, she made her way downstairs. Ravyn had become quite chubby after all of that time in the bedroom and not getting any exercise. Initially, it was hard for Ravyn to get up and down the stairs because she hadn't done it in such a long time. She takes those stairs like a champ now. After a while, Ravyn became a permanent fixture downstairs in the living room. She would lay under the coffee table, behind the couch, or on the ottoman. She loved to sunbathe on the floor near the window. And so, my mom started telling everyone that they had just gotten a cat. Even to this day, my mom thinks that Ravyn is a "baby." She has no idea that Ravyn is probably about fifteen years old. She has no idea where Ravyn came from or how she got there. She always tells the story about how she found Ravyn outside somewhere. She always says that Ravyn was so dirty and that her owners must not have taken care of her at all. Obviously, none of that is true, but you know what, it doesn't really matter, does it?

In the short amount of time since Dakota had passed away, we had accomplished a lot. I had been able to focus more on taking care of my mom and getting the house in order. Oakley had helped in getting my mom to spend more time outside. Ravyn had been rediscovered and given her freedom back. Later that summer, my mom and dad were even able to take a mini vacation to Cape May, NJ. This was something that they would have never been able to do while Dakota was still living because they couldn't leave him. I remember how excited they both were when they were planning the trip. They had planned to spend three nights in Cape May and my dad had reserved a fancy penthouse suite at some hotel. If anyone in the world deserved a vacation, it was my parents. I was willing to help in any way that I could to make their vacation possible.

I packed my mom's suitcase for her since she didn't know how to do it and my dad didn't have a clue what to pack for her. I had planned to clean their house and take care of Ravyn while they were away. I went over to their house two days in a row and cleaned all day long. It was not an easy task, but being there without my mom made it much easier to actually get everything done. I started with the bathrooms. They were pretty much a disaster. The sinks were all covered in pink soap scum and the toilets all had filthy rings around the bowls. The tubs and countertops were covered in dust bunnies. The shower in the guest bathroom had dead gnats all over the floor. The shower in the master bathroom had black gunk all along the tile and in the tracks of the shower doors. To put it bluntly, the bathrooms were all a filthy, unsanitary, disgusting mess. All I could think of was bleach, bleach, bleach, so I bleached, bleached, bleached. Those bathrooms were fucking immaculate when I was through with them. They had never shined so bright. I remember thinking how embarrassed and ashamed my mom would have felt at the condition of her house had it been just a few years earlier. She would have died if she ever saw her house that dirty. I just wanted to make it right for her. I put the same amount of effort into the kitchen, which I also felt was a filthy, unsanitary, disgusting mess. Then, I did a little dusting and vacuuming in the living room, dining room, family room, and all of the bedrooms. Finally, the house was clean. It was still extremely cluttered and disorganized, but it was clean.

While my parents were in Cape May, my dad was sending me pictures of what they were doing. He sent me pictures of them out to eat at restaurants and on a horse drawn carriage ride. They seemed to really be enjoying their trip. I'm sure that it was very difficult and a lot of work for my dad, but it still seemed like they were having a good time. I think it was good for them to get away for a few days. It would probably be the last good trip that they would ever be able to take together. When they got back, all my mom did was talk about their trip. She sounded really happy and seemed to have really enjoyed herself. My dad was amazed at how clean their house was when he saw it. I could tell that he was truly impressed by my hard work. It was like he thought I was some kind of miracle worker. All in all, I would say that their trip to Cape May was a success. They had a decent time and it gave me the opportunity to really clean their house the way it needed to be cleaned. They had so much fun, in fact, that they ended up not unpacking their suitcases until the following summer, when I finally did it for them.

It had been a crazy few months. From April to August, I had quit my job and started helping out at my parents' house, Dakota had been put down, Ravyn had been set free, the house had been cleaned and somewhat organized, and my parents had taken their first vacation in years. Aside from that, I had organized a relay team for the Delaware Marathon Running Festival to raise money for the Alzheimer's Association, we threw my parents a 45th wedding anniversary party, and I was training for my first half-marathon. There was definitely a lot going on at the time. All of these things made it difficult for me to notice any changes in my mom. I was spending more and more time with her, but that actually made it harder to see that her Alzheimer's was progressing. It's kind of like when someone loses a lot of weight, slowly, over a period of time. If you see that person every single day, then you're not as likely to notice the weight loss right away. But, if you haven't seen that person in a while, then you're likely to be blown away by their weight loss. It's like, "Goodbye, Fatty McButterpants! Somebody got skinny!" Most of the time, it was hard for me to see the changes in her. But sometimes, they jumped right out at me and smacked me across the face.

There were little things, like when my mom forgot who people were or where I went to college. These things jumped out at me all the time, but I felt that it was expected and it didn't bother me all that much. The bigger things were what really bothered me. I remember one day I was supposed to go to my mom's house with Oakley while my dad was at work. I had just called my mom to let her know that I was coming over, so that she wasn't startled when someone knocked at the door. When I got to my parents' house, Oakley and I went in through the garage and knocked on the door to the house. We were waiting there for a minute before my mom finally came to the door, unlocked it, and opened it. She saw that it was me, but she looked upset. With wide eyes, she put her finger up to her mouth as if to say, "Shhh!" I asked her what was going on. She said, "Shhh. There's a man in the house. I let him in. I thought he was one of us. He's still here." Ummm, excuse me? What the fuck? Both my mind and my heart started racing a mile a minute. I barged my way into the house with Oakley and told my mom to wait there. Oakley and I began to "clear" the house, as if I was a police officer and he was my canine partner, responding to a burglary in progress. Except, I was no longer a police officer, Oakley was not a police canine, and this was my parents' house. We went through the whole house. We checked every room, every closet, and underneath every bed. We checked the basement, to include the crawl space. There was no one there. There was no man in the house. There was no way that he could have gotten out without me seeing him. My mom must have hallucinated the whole thing.

I'm not going to lie. That scared the shit out of me. I don't ever remember being scared while clearing a house as a police officer. But this…this scared the shit out of me. Once I realized that there was no one in the house, I went to tell my mom that everything was ok. I actually felt bad having to tell her that there was no one in the house. I felt bad because then she would know that she had seen someone who wasn't even there. After I told her, I could tell that she felt stupid and embarrassed. I started asking her questions about what she had been doing before I arrived at her house. As it turns out, she was sitting in the chair in the family room, watching TV, and she had dozed off. When I knocked on the door, it must have startled her and she woke up. I believe that the man she thought she saw in the house was actually just a man that she had seen on the TV or in a reflection in the window. Since she had fallen asleep and was awoken so suddenly, I think that she was confused about what she had seen. Still, it scared me. It was a definite sign that her Alzheimer's was progressing.

There were some other big things that really jumped out at me and reminded me that my mom was constantly declining, even if I didn't notice it all the time. One time, I took my mom shopping at the mall and we decided to have lunch in the food court. Anyone who has ever been to the Christiana Mall knows that it is an absolute cluster fuck. I knew that the whole experience was probably very over-stimulating for my mom. I thought that I would try to make it easier for her by getting a table and having her wait there while I got our food. We found an open table near Saladworks, which is where we wanted to eat. I had my mom sit down and told her that I was going to get our food. I could see her the whole time while I waited in line, ordered, and paid for our food. I walked back to the table and started putting our stuff down. My mom looked right at me and said, "Oh no, I'm sorry. Someone is sitting here." Admittedly, I looked at her like she was crazy. She laughed awkwardly and said again, "I'm sorry. Someone is sitting here." I said, "Yeah, Mom, I know. I'm sitting here. It's me. Lauren." She looked scared momentarily and then tried to play it off. She said, "Yeah, I know." She laughed awkwardly again and tried to make a joke out of it. But, I knew that for one second, she looked at me, her own daughter, and didn't know who I was. She thought I was a stranger, who was trying to take her table in the food court at the Christiana Mall. Yeah, shit was definitely getting real.

With everything going on in my life, I was becoming increasingly overwhelmed, stressed out, and miserable. I thought that I could handle taking care of my mom. I thought that if anyone was strong enough to handle it, it was me. It was no big deal. I began to realize that I wasn't as strong as I had thought. It was very difficult for me to see that my mom's condition was worsening. It was also very difficult to be with her, day in and day out, helping take care of her. I left her house every day feeling physically and emotionally exhausted, defeated. I was completely drained. It was sucking the life out of me. To make matters worse, I still felt like no one could even begin to imagine what I was going through. I wasn't just hanging out with my mom every day and doing a little cleaning. I was watching the woman who had raised me slip away right before my eyes. She was becoming the child and I was becoming the mother. They always say that you find out who your true friends are when you're going through a difficult time in your life. Well, "they" are right. There's nothing like Alzheimer's to reveal a person's true colors and to show you who your real friends are.

Cutting out the Drama

I would say that my relationships with some of my friends started to unravel around the summer of 2011, shortly before my wedding. My friendships were never perfect to begin with, as there had been some ups and downs throughout the years, but that's to be expected. I had met two of my best friends during my freshman year in college. We had all been inseparable during those four years. We had always either been roommates, apartment-mates, or across-the-hall-mates. After graduation, we remained good friends, although we obviously didn't see each other nearly as much as we had in college. Once I started the police academy, I was definitely MIA most of the time. The police academy consumed my life for a solid six months. Once I graduated, I started working full time and I was on rotating shift work. I worked different days and a different shift each week. I rarely ever had nights or weekends off and forget about the holidays. Still, we made it work and saw each other as much as we could.

My best friend at the time was getting married just five months before my wedding. I was in her wedding and she was in mine. I decided to have a small bridal party because I wanted to keep it as manageable as possible. Being that my mom had been diagnosed with Alzheimer's during the same month that I had gotten engaged, I already had a lot on my plate. I didn't want to have a bunch of bitchy bridesmaids to deal with on top of everything else. My sister, my future sister-in-law, and my best friend were the only bridesmaids. My future sister-in-law lived in New Jersey, so she wasn't always around to help with the planning for the bridal shower and the bachelorette party. That left my sister and my best friend, who had never really liked each other, to plan everything together. They had always talked about each other to me over the years. I was a little worried, but I figured that they would figure it out or my sister would enlist some of her other friends to help her with the planning.

Well, my sister and my best friend did more than just figure it out. They actually became friends and started hanging out with each other to plan the wedding events. In theory, I should have been relieved and happy about this, but I wasn't. My sister is only eleven months older than me. I had grown up having to share everything with my sister and I felt like I was always in her shadow. I always preferred to have my own friends and not to share them with my sister. It just made me happier to have some parts of my life that were my own, separate from hers. My best friend had always known this and seemed to understand it. When the two of them started becoming so chummy, it really bothered me. I wanted them to get along, but I didn't necessarily want them to be besties.

I tried really hard to let it go and to accept their new friendship, but I just couldn't seem to do it. I thought that maybe their friendship would fade away once my wedding was over and there wasn't anything left to plan, but it didn't. They actually became even better friends. I felt like it happened over night, behind my back. Apparently, they were hanging out all the time while I was at work. It had gotten to the point where they had made plans and I wasn't even invited. Most of the time, I didn't even find out about their plans until they were over with. I would always find out after the fact that they had done something together. Where the fuck was my invite? They always claimed that they had just assumed that I had to work or that I wouldn't be interested in what they had planned to do. Since I didn't drink and their plans often involved drinking, they just assumed that I wouldn't want to go. I wasn't even given the option of declining an invitation because I was never invited in the first place. It seemed like the only things I was invited to were parties, which everyone was invited to. I began to feel so uncomfortable and out of place around the two of them that I always came up with an excuse as to why I couldn't hang out. And then, they had the audacity to get upset with me when I didn't come to something. They wanted to pick and choose what they invited me to and then they got mad at me when I said I couldn't come.

This went on for a while and only continued to get worse. After I decided to quit my job, I thought that my friendships would improve because I would be around more. I made an effort to hang out with my friends more often, but I always ended up feeling like an outsider. I felt like my friends and my sister had all of these memories and inside jokes that I wasn't a part of. I felt like when we were all together, all they did was talk about all of their memories and inside jokes. I felt like they were trying to make me jealous or rub it in my face that they had all become such good friends. I usually sat there all night feeling miserable and excluded. I was always the first one to leave because I couldn't wait to get the hell out of there. That's how uncomfortable I had become around my own friends. The friends that I had known for about ten years. I felt like a complete outsider. I couldn't stand to be around them anymore. I avoided hanging out with them as much as I possibly could. I admittedly gave them one bullshit excuse after another as to why I couldn't hang out. Spending time with them wasn't worth the misery I would feel when I left. I had enough to be upset and stressed out about with my mom. I didn't need to add to it.

I took a huge step back from my friendships. I felt as though my two best friends had almost completely dropped me for my sister. I felt like they all expected a lot from me, but none of them were willing to do the same for me in return. Once I stopped catering to them and bending over backward to spend time with them, I became the bad guy. They all talked about me and how I had "changed." They talked about the fact that I didn't drink like it was a bad thing. They talked about how they all felt like I gave them bullshit excuses as to why I couldn't hang out. Like I said, I admittedly gave them bullshit excuses, but no one seemed to care why I was giving them bullshit excuses. I completely withdrew myself from the group and no one really seemed to care. I was drowning in sorrow, loneliness, and depression, but no one even seemed to notice. If they did, then they just didn't care enough to talk to me about it. They were all too busy hanging out and drinking with each other.

My best friend did call me once to talk about what was going on. Her husband had given her a surprise 29th birthday party on a Friday night and I didn't go. I knew I had to spend the entire day Saturday with her and my sister because we were picking out bridesmaid dresses for my other best friend's wedding. My other friend had asked both me and my sister to be in her wedding. The whole thing was just annoying to me and I was getting really stressed out about it. My other friend decided to have a surprise 35th birthday party for her fiancé on Saturday night. I really didn't want to spend Friday night, all day Saturday, and Saturday night with these people. I just couldn't stomach being around them and all of their fakeness anymore. I always felt like they were throwing their friendship in my face. Plus, who the fuck has a surprise 29th or 35th birthday party? It's not like 29 is a milestone birthday, unless you're dying or something and every year that you live is a miracle. Get over yourselves. But that's just me.

So anyway, my best friend called me and wanted to talk about things. She started off the conversation by saying that she thought I should know that I had hurt a lot of people's feelings. Excuse me? *I* had hurt *their* feelings? What about *my* feelings? It seemed as though no one cared about my feelings. She even admitted that she knew that her friendship with my sister would probably upset me, but she thought that I would just get over it. In other words, she knew that what she was doing was going to hurt me, but she just didn't care. It didn't help things when she then had the audacity to question me about my relationship with my own sister and to ask me whether or not I had "yelled" at her during a specific conversation. She was *my sister*. I had the right to confront her about something if it was bothering me. Whatever I discussed with my sister was none of my friend's business. It was not her place to get involved. Who the hell did she think she was? I should've just been honest with her instead of trying to make nice with her. What she didn't realize was that I was completely checked out of the friendship at that point. The damage had already been done. I was just trying to get through my other friend's wedding before I cut everyone out completely.

I remember some people saying that I was just jealous of my sister's friendship with my best friend. Well, I can tell you that I didn't feel jealous. I felt hurt and betrayed. It wasn't just that my sister had started hanging out with my friends. It wasn't just that she had become a part of the group. She had taken my place in the group. My best friends had replaced me with my sister. I had become the outsider, the plus one. Nothing about that felt right to me. I felt like I had been stepped on, disrespected. All of my boundaries had been crossed. My feelings had been deeply hurt. But, as long as everyone else got what they wanted, my feelings didn't seem to matter.

For me, it was a question of loyalty and respect. My best friend had known me for over ten years. She knew how I felt and seemed to understand and accept it. She had always agreed with me. Until she didn't. Then it was as if she expected me to just suddenly stop feeling the way I had always felt because it didn't suit her anymore. Just because she suddenly stopped understanding and accepting how I felt, it didn't mean that I suddenly stopped feeling that way. How can you be best friends with someone for so long and have such a total disregard for her feelings? How can you just drop her for someone who is more fun, especially during a time in her life when she needs you the most? Where is your loyalty? Loyalty and respect are big for me in all of my relationships. Once I realized that my best friends had no loyalty for me and no respect for my feelings, I knew the friendships were over.

Aside from dropping me for my sister, I was disappointed in my two best friends because I felt like they weren't really there for me when it came to my mom. I didn't expect them to call me every day and ask me how she was doing, but I felt like they rarely asked at all. Whenever I did talk to them about it, I felt like they didn't really want to hear about it because it was too sad. They never asked me how I was doing or how I was handling it. They never offered to help. They almost acted as if there was nothing going on. I don't know if it was because talking about it made them uncomfortable or they just didn't know what to say. I don't think they realized the reality and the brutality of what I was going through with my mom. They didn't realize how depressed, lost, confused, overwhelmed, and stressed out I was at the time. They just didn't get it. But, they didn't even try to get it. They rarely ever brought it up.

I never told my two best friends what was going on anyway. I felt like they wouldn't understand, so I just didn't tell them anything. My sister told them everything. They were always finding out about stuff from her first. When my parents' dog, Dakota, wasn't doing well, I never mentioned it to my best friend. It was something that my family had to deal with. My sister told my best friend that Dakota wasn't doing well and that my parents were starting to think about putting him down. When this was all going on, I was going over to my parents' house almost every day to help out. One day, I was getting ready to go to their house when I got a text message from my best friend. She said that she had heard from my sister that Dakota wasn't doing well. When I initially read the text, I thought that my best friend was offering to come over to my parents' house to help me organize some stuff. I thought that was really sweet of her to offer to help me. However, when I re-read the text, I realized that

I had misread it. She had actually asked me if I wanted to come to *her* house to help *her* organize a closet or two. She figured that I would want to be close to home in case something happened with Dakota. What the fuck?

First of all, she lived at least twenty minutes away from me, which I didn't consider to be all that close. Second of all, how the hell would organizing her closets be helpful to my parents or me in any way? And finally, what the hell did any of that have to do with Dakota not doing well? "Oh, I heard that your family dog is about to die. Why don't you help me organize my house in case something happens to him?" I think I literally laughed out loud to myself when I realized what the text actually said. Bitch, please. I don't even have time to clean my own house, let alone help you organize your fucking closets.

It was things like that a million times over and the realization that I stressed about my friendships more than I enjoyed them that made me finally end them. All I did was go over and over everything in my head, trying to decide what I should do. My poor husband. He listened to me bitch, complain, and over-analyze things for three years. I finally realized that just because they had been my friends for a long time, that didn't make them good friends and it was no reason to keep them as friends. My friendships no longer met my definition of the word "friendship." My relationships with my friends had become toxic. I'm not saying that these friends were bad people. A friend can be a good person, while also being a toxic person in your life. My friendships were causing me more bad than good at that point. It was time to move on and so I did.

In the end, I did it abruptly and somewhat anti-climatically. I called my friend and dropped out of her wedding. Maybe I was wrong for doing that, but I didn't care anymore. I was standing up for myself and protecting myself. No one else even bothered to call me and ask why I dropped out. I didn't have the energy to call my best friend and explain it to her, so I just literally never spoke to her again. She didn't bother to call me either. I had a lot of bigger things to worry about. All of this drama had been distracting me and shifting my focus away from my mom. If they didn't get that, there was nothing I could do to make them understand.

I think it's true what people say about Alzheimer's. It really does drive people away. People are afraid of it. They don't understand it. They don't know how to deal with it. And, they don't want to deal with it because it's just too sad. When my friends found out that my mom had Alzheimer's, they didn't all rally together to support me. When someone is dying of cancer, it's not uncommon for that person's friends, family, and neighbors to come together to support him/her. Everyone stops by the house to visit or to drop off meals. Everyone wants to help in any way that they can. Everyone wants to talk about it and ask how the person is doing. It's not like that when someone is dying of Alzheimer's. No one stops by to visit. No one drops off meals. No one really offers to do anything at all. No one wants to talk about it because it is too sad. It is the elephant in the room. I never really expected my friends to react in that way, but when they didn't, it definitely caused a lot of resentment toward them.

I don't think my friends back then even knew the extent of my sadness and depression. They didn't know how all-consuming my mom's Alzheimer's was for me. It wasn't like she was getting noticeably worse by the day. It wasn't like something bad or scary was happening to her every day. She had never been in the hospital because of her Alzheimer's. It wasn't like she was going to die tomorrow. But, I thought about her Alzheimer's all day, every single day. I wasn't sad all day, every day, but there was definitely a lot of sadness in each day. I was consumed by my mom's Alzheimer's. It didn't matter that I wasn't with her all the time or that there were days in a row when I didn't see her at all. She was always with me in my mind, heart, and soul. I didn't think about anything else. I was drowning, weighed down by a brick of Alzheimer's that was sitting on my chest. No one knew because no one asked. It didn't matter though. There was nothing they could have done to help. They didn't have a cure. I just knew that I had to free myself from anything else in my life that was weighing me down. I had to free myself from all of the drama and negativity. It was the only chance I had to survive.

Should I Stay or Should I Go?

Setting myself free from my toxic friendships was the first step in beginning to live my life for me. I had realized that over the years I had developed a tendency to do whatever everyone else wanted me to do instead of what I really wanted to do. I guess I was a bit of a people pleaser. I had a really hard time telling people "no." I actually think that this is a common problem among women in general. For me, it was time to stop trying to please everyone and to start trying to please myself. I had been in a very dark, lonely, sad place for a few years now. My mom was diagnosed with Alzheimer's in July 2010, which was also when I got engaged. In 2011, I bought a house, got a dog, and got married. In 2012, I was struggling to keep my head above water. The storm was raging full force, with the winds gusting and the flood waters rising. I was in deep. By April 2013, I had finally decided to quit my job and I took on the role of a part-time caregiver for my mom. I watched the woman who raised me slowly and painfully disappear right before my own eyes. I was mourning her loss, but she was still living. No one knew what I was going through. By the end of 2013 into the beginning of 2014, I had finally begun to stand up for myself and to protect myself from anything that was doing me harm. I had done enough harm to myself over the past three years. In April 2014, I ended two friendships that had lasted over ten years. Now, it was definitely time for me to "find myself" and start living my life for me.

In trying to "find myself," I registered for classes at the community college to pursue a vet-tech degree. I wasn't even sure that I wanted to be a vet-tech, but I felt like I had to do something. I wasn't working. I wasn't going to school. I felt like I had nothing to show for myself. So, I registered for two classes for the spring 2014 semester. During that semester, all I did was homework, study, or bitch about homework and studying. I ended up getting an A in both classes, but it was definitely a lot of work. It was more work than I ever remembered doing during my four years of undergrad, when I had a double major and a minor. I realized that the last thing I wanted to do was go back to school. I had done enough homework and had studied for enough tests in my life. It was going to take me at least three years to get an associate's degree to become a vet-tech. I was worried that once I finished school and got a job in the field, I wouldn't even like it. I mean, I had wanted to be a police officer since I was about five years old. When I finally became one, I hated it more than anything in the world. I really didn't want that to happen again. Plus, during that one easy semester, I barely saw my mom. If I wasn't in class or lab, I was doing housework, homework, or studying. I didn't have any extra time to go over to my parents' house to help out like I had been doing. I felt extremely guilty about it. I had to decide what I really wanted to do with my life.

There was also another big decision that I had to make. My husband had always dreamed of becoming a helicopter pilot for the Army. He had served on active duty from 2003-2007 and then got out of the Army to become a police officer. He always talked about going back into the Army to become a pilot. He talked about it from the first day I met him. I would always blow him off and tell him that he couldn't go back in the Army because we were both police officers in Delaware. I told him that I didn't want him to leave me when he inevitably got deployed. He continued to talk about it anyway. He always said that it was his dream job. Once I quit the police department, I was running out of excuses for him not to pursue his dream. We talked about it all the time. I realized that I didn't have any right to deny him the opportunity of pursuing his dream job. I had always wished that I had a clear-cut, dream job in my mind. I didn't, but he did. I didn't think that it was right for me to tell him that he couldn't follow his dreams. I didn't want to be the reason that he never achieved his dream of becoming a pilot.

After many discussions with my husband and endless hours of thinking about it on my own, I finally gave my husband my blessing to pursue becoming a helicopter pilot. We compromised on him enlisting in the Delaware Army National Guard, rather than active duty, because I wanted to be able to stay close to my mom and not have to move around all the time. We decided that the only way he would enlist was if he was able to ensure that he would get a spot to go to flight school. He did. It took a while to work everything out and to process the paperwork, but he signed papers and took his oath on December 30, 2013. He immediately completed his flight school packet and began the process to be officially selected for flight school. They were able to rush his packet through to ensure that he would get the one open spot that was available that year for flight school. He was officially selected in May 2014. In June 2014, he would leave to begin his training at Fort Rucker, Alabama. The initial part of the training lasted five weeks and I was unable to go with him, as he would be living in barracks. Then, he would come home for three weeks before he went back to Fort Rucker at the end of August to continue his training, which would last at least one year. I had to decide whether or not I was going to move to Alabama with him in August. The move would be temporary and we would move back to Delaware once he graduated from flight school. We were told to expect to be in Alabama for twelve to fourteen months. So, should I stay or should I go?

I thought about my decision all the time. I was constantly weighing the pros and cons in my head. While I thought it would be great for me to get away from home and all my problems for a year or more, I also thought it would be really wrong for me to leave my mom and dad for that long. I thought that moving to Alabama would give me the distance, space, and time that I needed to "find myself," but I was also afraid of losing time with my mom. I also knew that it would be really difficult to live away from my husband for over a year, especially when I had the chance to go with him. I couldn't begin to imagine what it would be like to only talk to him on the phone and see him every few months. Realistically, we wouldn't be able to visit all that often because we would both be busy living our lives. Our own, separate lives. I was afraid that we would grow apart and that I would end up resenting him for leaving me to go to flight school. I knew that if I went with him, then I would be there to help and support him while he pursued his lifelong dream of becoming a pilot. But, I also knew that I would be alone a lot because he would be very busy with his training. I was constantly going back and forth on my decision. I thought I had made up my mind, but then I thought of another pro or con and changed my mind again. I just didn't know what to do.

One reoccurring thought that I had was, "How can I leave my mom now while she still knows who I am?" I was terrified that if I moved to Alabama, I would go home to see my mom one day and she would not recognize me. I thought that if that ever happened, I would instantly regret my decision to move to Alabama with my husband. If that ever happened, I would think that it was my fault for moving away from her. That I had brought it on myself. But then, I realized the reality was that there would come a day when she did not recognize my face. That day would come no matter what. There was no stopping it or controlling when it came. It would come whether I lived in Alabama or in Delaware. It would come whether I saw her every two months or every single day. It would come even if I spent every waking, living, breathing moment of my life right by her side. It was going to happen and I couldn't do a damn thing about it. It was all part of this horrific, gut-wrenching, disgusting disease. There was nothing anyone could do to stop it.

I had two choices. I could sit around with my mom, waiting for her to forget me, while growing apart from my husband and possibly destroying my marriage. Or, I could continue to go on living my life with my husband and best friend, figure out who I was and what I wanted out of life, and come home with a plan. I could either let Alzheimer's take control of my life or I could live my life. I decided to live it. I wanted to be there to support my husband. I knew that my mom would have wanted me to be with him. Of all people, she would have understood, even if she didn't really understand. She loved her husband more than anyone in the world. She always wanted to be with him, near him. She knew how important it was for a husband and wife to be together. She would have wanted me to go with my husband. She would have wanted me to live my life. *I* wanted to live my life. A life my mom would be proud of. She would eventually forget who I was, but I couldn't allow myself to forget, too. I couldn't stand the thought of ending up a divorced and alone 40-something, with no job, no family, and no life, one day when my mom was no longer around. I would have nothing to show for my life. Like I said earlier, it was time for me to start living my life for me. It was time to start worrying less about pleasing everyone else and more about pleasing myself. I wanted to do what I wanted to do for a change. And, I can't believe I'm saying this but, I wanted to move to Alabama.

When I finally made the decision to go with my husband to Alabama, I was consumed with guilt. I felt like everyone was going to judge me for leaving my family at such a delicate time. "How could she leave her mom like that?" "What if her mom forgets who she is when she comes back?" "Who is going to help her dad out now that she isn't around?" I am sure that some people had those exact thoughts when they found out that I was moving to Alabama. Hell, I had those exact thoughts and, at times, I still feel that way. I was very indecisive about whether or not to move to Alabama. It was not an easy decision for me to make. But, I decided that I wanted a long-lasting, loving, and supportive marriage. I could not imagine being away from my husband and best friend during such a monumental point in his life. He was going to follow a dream that he always had and I wanted to be by his side through it all. If I had chosen to stay in Delaware, I would have probably ended up moving down to Alabama anyway. My husband is my absolute best friend. Home is wherever he is. But that wasn't enough to make the guilt go away.

Caring for a loved one with Alzheimer's creates an environment that perpetuates a constant state of guilt. I felt guilty that I didn't spend enough time with my mom. I felt guilty that I didn't do enough to help out with her and my dad. I felt guilty that I didn't call her every single day. When I did spend time with her, I calculated the hours/minutes that I spent and it never seemed like enough. Same thing with our phone calls. I actually looked at the duration of the call on my call log to see if the conversation was long enough. It never was. When I was home in Delaware, I went over to my parents' house frequently to help clean or just to spend time with my mom. Even then, it was never enough. I should have cleaned more. I should have stayed longer. I should have taken her somewhere. When I did spend all day with her or take her somewhere, I felt incredibly guilty for being so impatient with her or snapping at her. To add to all of that guilt, I felt guilty spending so much time with her when I should have been spending time doing other things. Cleaning, laundry, grocery shopping, running, working out, or spending time with my husband and Oakley. Or, just simply figuring out what I wanted to do with my life. Guilt on top of guilt on top of more guilt. It was never ending.

I soon realized that the constant feeling of guilt would remain regardless of what state I lived in. I could have moved into my parents' house and been with my mom 24/7. I would have still found something to feel guilty about. Nothing that I did would ever be enough because it wouldn't cure my mom's Alzheimer's. I wasn't going to find a cure. Not in Delaware. Not in Alabama. No matter where I lived, no matter what I did, my mom would never be the same again. I was going to have to learn to accept that at some point. I wasn't there yet, but I knew I would get there some day. For now, I would just have to accept the guilt, carry its weight on my own two shoulders, and move on.

Speaking of moving on, I decided to move on from my decision to go back to school. I realized that I didn't actually want to be going to school. I hated having to do all of the homework and studying. It was very time-consuming. Not to mention that a majority of the classes I would be required to take had absolutely nothing to do with being a vet-tech. It didn't matter that I had already taken most of those classes during my four years of undergrad. I would have to take them again anyway. Nope. I was over it. The moment had passed. School was definitely not for me anymore.

Based on my husband's orders for flight school, I knew that I would be living in Alabama by the end of the summer of 2014. There was no way I would even consider enrolling in classes for the summer or fall, knowing that I had already decided to move to Alabama with my husband. I decided that it would be ridiculous for me to try to find a job since I would be leaving in just a few months. I really needed that time to get things in order and start packing. My husband agreed that it would be silly to stress over finding a job, work there for a few months, and then quit to move to Alabama. I decided to talk to my dad about "working" for him again. He agreed to compensate me for helping out around the house and with my mom. I was happy knowing that I would be able to bring Oakley with me every day and I was also glad that I would get to spend a lot of time with my parents before I moved. However, I was a little unsure of going back to my caregiving role, especially since my husband would be gone for five weeks to begin his training in Alabama. He was my rock and confidante. Who was I going to lean on for support while he was away? Plus, we had never been apart for more than a night, so I was worried about how I was going to handle him being away. We would be lucky if we were allowed to talk on the phone once a week. Since we had never been through that before, I didn't know how I was going to feel. I was afraid that between taking care of my mom and missing my husband, I was going to fall apart. But, I was about to find out that I was one pretty tough bitch.

Holding It Down

My husband left to begin his training at the end of June 2014. I was very sad in the days leading up to his departure. I began to miss him before he even left. I would sit there looking at his bags, packed and ready to go, and I would start tearing up. I was also very nervous and anxious for him to leave. I've always said that saying goodbye is the hardest part. I hate the build-up and the production of it. Part of me couldn't wait for him to leave just so that the goodbye part would be over with. On the day he left, we had to wake up at 2:00am so that I could drive him to the airport. I was very sad, but surprisingly calm the entire way to the airport. Once we got there and I pulled over to drop him off, I started bawling my eyes out. We brought our dog, Oakley, with us so that my husband could say goodbye to him, too. It definitely helped having Oakley there, but I still couldn't stop crying. I know my husband felt bad leaving me like that, but he had to go. And, just like that, he was off. See ya in five weeks!

Oakley and I drove home and took a nap together on the couch. I woke up feeling so sad and missing my husband so much. I didn't want to be alone, so I ended up spending the whole day at my parents' house and had dinner there. The day went on and on. It was the longest day of my life. We didn't really have anything to do or anywhere to go. I really wasn't in the mood to do anything or go anywhere anyway. We just spent the day hanging out at their house, sitting on the back porch. I was crying off and on all day. My mom didn't really understand why I was so upset. I had to keep explaining to her that my husband had just left for five weeks and that I was sad because I was going to miss him. I must have explained it to her at least ten times. She either didn't understand what was happening or she just forgot. Then, out of nowhere, my mom had a moment of pure clarity. I was talking about how much I was going to miss my husband because he wasn't there with me. She said, "Steve is always with you. He might not be here, but he is in *here*," and she put her hand over her heart. I started crying again, but they were happy tears this time. I was so proud of my mom for being able to speak so clearly and so profoundly. I knew that she was right. My husband was always in my heart. I knew that the next five weeks would fly by.

As the days went on, I began to feel much better. I still missed my husband, but I wasn't sad anymore. I knew that if I just kept myself busy, the time would be over before I knew it. By the end of the first week, I was fine and the countdown was on. I kept busy by running, working out, taking care of my mom, and spending time with my friends. I spent most of my time with my mom. We went shopping, out to lunch, got our hair done, took walks at the park with Oakley, and swam in my parents' pool. My mom loved to watch Oakley swim in the pool. All I had to do was throw his tennis ball into the pool. Oakley would come running up onto the pool deck and jump into the pool to get his ball. My mom thought it was the best thing in the world. She would laugh and laugh as she watched him jump in, swim to his ball, and bring it back out. My mom thought that Oakley just ran and jumped into the pool on his own, like he had broken in or something. She didn't realize that I was throwing the ball into the pool in order to get him to go swimming in it. It never got old for her. She could watch Oakley swim all day long.

Aside from the fun stuff, I was doing a lot of actual work, too. I was doing the laundry, cleaning the house, making lunch, and "babysitting" my mom. I would stay with her so that my dad could go to work for a few hours. Most of the time, my mom would just sit and watch TV while I cleaned or did the laundry. She was constantly asking me why I was doing her laundry and cleaning her house. I didn't want her to be offended so I would always ask her if she wanted to help me. She usually said that she didn't really feel like cleaning. She never wanted to help me or let me show her how to do it herself. I hated feeling like I was my mom's cleaning lady. There were some days that I would be at her house for hours cleaning and helping out, but I had minimal interaction with my mom. I would get her a drink or something to eat. I would help her get to the bathroom. But, other than that, she sat around while I did all the work.

I tried to find activities for us to do that she could be involved in. She never wanted to clean or do the laundry, but she would help with other things sometimes. One day we planted flowers in flower pots together. I gave my mom the job of watering all of the flowers. I made a big deal about how important it was for her to water the flowers. She did a great job and I could tell that she was really proud of herself. It made her feel useful and she was happy to be able to contribute something to our project. Other times, when I was upstairs cleaning or doing laundry, I would ask her to watch Oakley for me. He would usually just run around in the back yard or lay on the back porch. I knew that he didn't really need to be watched, but it made my mom feel useful. They would just sit on the back porch together. A woman and her grand-dog. I loved watching them together and my mom felt like she was really helping me out. I longed for more times like that, but she often didn't want to help me do anything. It was difficult to motivate her.

There were days when I thought I couldn't take it anymore. I would sit and look at my mom, trying to figure out what she was thinking about. Trying to solve the Alzheimer's puzzle. I was doing my best to help take care of her and to help my dad around the house, but it never felt like I was doing enough. I wanted to figure

105

her out. I wanted to find a way to make her life more meaningful. There were many days when I would leave her house feeling completely defeated. Days when I would realize that all I had really done was babysit my mom all day. We watched TV all day and accomplished nothing. We were lucky to just get through the day. Alzheimer's had won again.

On these days, I would go home and want nothing more than to vent to my husband about how much I hated stupid fucking Alzheimer's. Of course, I couldn't do that since my husband was away. I couldn't even pick up the phone to call him and vent to him. I couldn't text him or e-mail him. I realized that I couldn't always rely on him to be there when I needed him. As I've previously said, I'm not the type of person to call my friends and bitch about my problems. I never wanted to be the whiny friend who was always complaining about her life and her problems. No one wanted to hear that shit. So, I quickly learned that I would have to rely on myself to deal with my problems. I wanted to be strong enough to stand on my own, even though I knew I wouldn't always have to. I wanted to be the embodiment of a strong, independent woman. I knew I had it in me, but I had never had the necessity to do it all on my own. This was a chance for me to prove myself to myself. It was time to man up.

If I had a bad day at my parents' house, I would come home to my empty house and deal with it. If I had to sit down and cry for a while, I sat down and cried for a while. If I had to take a long, hot shower, I took a long, hot shower. I know this sounds crazy, but I would often just vent to myself. I would talk out loud, to myself, in my empty house, about whatever was bothering me. Sometimes it was just what I needed to do to get it all out. At the time, it never occurred to me to write about it, so I would just talk to myself about it. I always listened to myself and agreed with myself so I always felt better when I was done venting to myself. Besides, Oakley was always there to listen. Even if he couldn't understand what I was saying, he knew how I was feeling. He was a permanent fixture right by my side. He followed me around the house. He was always willing to listen as long as we could cuddle afterward. I spent every night of those five weeks snuggling with my little boy. He truly was my soul mate.

Between long showers, venting to myself, and cuddling with Oakley, I was able to handle any shitty day that came my way. It also helped that I have always been a gym rat and an avid runner. I would either go to the gym or go for a run every morning. It was my therapy. There was nothing that a good workout couldn't fix. I began to feel very strong. And, I don't just mean physically strong, but emotionally strong, as well. I was holding shit down while my husband was away. I took care of myself, Oakley, the house, and my mom, as well as her house. I did all of the cleaning, paid the bills, cut the grass, and handled anything that came up. I spent every night alone. If I heard a noise in the middle of the night or Oakley started barking at something, I grabbed my gun and checked the house. I know many women who are afraid to spend the night alone in their own house. I have never been that girl, but it still felt good to prove to myself that I wasn't that girl. I did everything on my own. Anything that needed to be done, I did it. It felt great. I was proving to myself that I was a strong, independent woman, who didn't fall apart without her husband.

It was this strong, independent woman attitude that enabled me to do something amazing. With my new-found strength, I was able to stop feeling sorry for myself. I was able to ditch the whole "woe is me" attitude. I had never wanted to be that type of person. The type of person who feels so sorry for herself that she is only able to think about herself and her problems. I never wanted to be that sad, sorry, self-pitying type of person. But, somehow, I had become the exact type of person that I never wanted to be. I spent the first few years after my mom's diagnosis wallowing in self-pity and crying about every little thing. I couldn't even look at my mom without my eyes filling up with tears. Whenever I was around her, I felt nothing but sadness and pity for myself. I would often have to go into another room to cry. Part of it was feeling the sadness of watching her decline, but a bigger part was feeling sorry for myself at what I was going through with her Alzheimer's. I couldn't stand myself anymore. I had become so weak. I had allowed my mom's Alzheimer's to take over my whole life and to change me as a person. Finding my strength and independence that summer allowed me to put an end to my pity party.

I realized that I knew plenty of people whose lives were a lot worse than mine. Plenty of people whose loved ones had died from or were currently suffering from other illnesses just as bad as, if not worse than, Alzheimer's. Plenty of people who lost their mothers and fathers at a young age. I was lucky to have had twenty-five years with my mom before I started losing her. I also realized that I would never be able to take good care of my mom if I just sat around feeling sorry for myself all the time. How was I ever going to see things clearly if my eyes were constantly filled with tears? How was I ever going to be able to solve the Alzheimer's puzzle and figure my mom out? I was tired of crying all the time. I was stronger than that. So, I gave myself a reality check. I told myself that it could always be worse. I told myself that I should be grateful for my mom and the time that I had left with her. I told myself that my mom was the one who was suffering the most and that I needed to be strong for her.

Once I dried my tears, I would be able to be present in the moment when I was with my mom. I would be able to focus on her and taking care of her because I wasn't too busy feeling sorry for myself anymore. There were going to be good days and bad days. I realized that I didn't need to break down and sob uncontrollably every time there was a bad day. Tomorrow would be a new day and I would do my best to make it a good one. There were often signs that my mom's Alzheimer's was progressing. There was no need for me to sink into a deep, dark hole of self-pity every time she did something that made me realize she was getting worse. What the fuck did I expect to happen? She had a disease for which there was no treatment and no cure. Of course it was going to get worse and continue to get worse without giving up. I should expect to see signs that she was declining. As soon as I realized and accepted all of these things, I was able to stop feeling sorry for myself and move on. I was able to become a better caregiver for my mom.

I went from crying every time I looked at my mom to crying every once in a while. I shifted my focus from how my mom's Alzheimer's was affecting *me* to how it was affecting *her*. I was able to see Alzheimer's more clearly now. I was beginning to try to understand it. To solve the puzzle. What things were my mom still capable of doing? What things were totally out of the question? Were my expectations of her too high? What should I expect from her? These were all questions that I began to ask myself. It seems kind of crazy, but I had never thought about these things before. I had always been too busy feeling sorry for myself and being sad. When I had played the caregiver role in the past, I spent most of the time just babysitting my mom and cleaning up her house. I guess I always had more of a reactive approach than a proactive one. I had always allowed my mom's Alzheimer's to control us rather than us trying to control it. I had allowed Alzheimer's to dictate our days together rather than us deciding how we wanted to spend them.

I realized that I needed to change my approach. Rather than simply reacting to my mom's Alzheimer's, I had to try to find a way to get ahead of it. I had to try to predict what was going to happen or how she was going to react ahead of time. I had to be prepared. When the weather forecast predicts that a bad storm is approaching, you don't just sit there and wait for it to hit you. You prepare for it. You head indoors for shelter. You secure your house and items in your backyard. You have flashlights, candles, water, and food ready to go. You might even develop a safety plan with your family if the storm is going to be really severe. Well, Alzheimer's is one hell of a fucking storm. I needed to start preparing myself for it instead of letting it wreak havoc on my life. I needed to start learning how to weather the storm.

Obviously, this didn't happen overnight. There were a lot of pieces to this puzzle. I needed time to start putting them all together. Changing my approach to my mom's Alzheimer's would happen little by little, day by day, as I learned more about it. Alzheimer's was constantly throwing new scenarios at me. No two days were the same. I was going to have to learn as I went along. I could learn from my mistakes in order to prevent making the same ones over and over again. The point is that I found my strength that summer. My strength allowed me to stop feeling sorry for myself. And, once I stopped feeling sorry for myself, I started paying attention to what was really important; my mom. I developed a new attitude and a new approach. I started thinking, asking questions, and learning more about Alzheimer's. I was determined to learn how to weather the storm.

Sweet Home Alabama

My husband completed the initial phase of his training at the end of July 2014. Then, he came home for three weeks before we were scheduled to move to Fort Rucker, Alabama. During those three weeks, we packed and organized for our trip to Alabama. We spent a lot of time with our friends and family, knowing that it would be a while before we would see them again. I was very excited to move to Alabama. Other than during my four years of college, I had never lived outside of Delaware. I never had the experience of moving to a new city, in a new state, and starting all over. I was excited to have new surroundings and to make new friends. I was excited to explore a new area. I was excited to have a new beginning and a much-needed break from Alzheimer's. And, I was so excited for my husband to begin flight school. I was so proud of him for all that he had already accomplished and all that he would accomplish in the future. He was chasing his dreams and I couldn't have been happier for him.

Along with that happiness came a lot of sadness, anxiety, and guilt. I was sad to be leaving my friends and family, especially my parents. I was sad that I wasn't going to be able to drive over to my parents' house whenever I wanted to see them. I was sad that I wasn't going to see my mom for months at a time. I had a lot of anxiety about the move itself and the logistics of everything. The drive to Alabama was about sixteen hours long for us and we decided to break it up into a couple of days so that we could take our time getting there. I was nervous about what our on-post housing would look like. I was anxious to get there, get settled in, and unpack everything. I was also very nervous about meeting new people and making new friends. I hadn't really made any new friends since college. I met a lot of new people through my job at the police department, but no one that I really considered to be a friend. I had plenty of acquaintances, but not many real friends. I was nervous because I did not consider myself to be a typical girl. I hated wearing nice clothes and doing my hair and makeup. I didn't want to cook, do crafts, or be around a bunch of kids. I didn't have any kids of my own and I didn't want any. If I wasn't running or at the gym, I was hanging out with my dog. I was afraid that I wasn't going to fit in or make any friends. That would make for a very lonely year in Alabama.

Worse than the sadness and anxiety was the extreme guilt that I felt. I felt so incredibly guilty that I was going to be leaving my parents for over a year. I felt like I was abandoning them and forcing them to deal with my mom's Alzheimer's on their own. I had been the only one helping out with my mom and giving my dad a break from all of the stress. Everyone else was too busy with work and their own families to really be available to help out. I was the only one that was both available and willing to help. I was at my parents' house almost every day that summer helping out. What the hell was my dad going to do once I was gone? Who was going to help him out? I didn't know and I felt so bad about leaving him stranded like that. I tried to convince him to hire someone to help out before I left. I thought it would be a good time to bring someone in because I would still be there for a couple of weeks to help them get settled. My dad was very resistant to hiring outside help because he felt as though my mom wouldn't like it. He thought that she would get upset and mad at him if he hired outside help. I did what I could to try to convince him, but it didn't work. Even though it was his decision to not get help, I still felt consumed with guilt that he wouldn't have anyone there to help him out. I truly felt as though I was abandoning him and leaving him stranded. I felt like it was all my fault.

Still, I had already made the decision to move to Alabama with my husband and I was sticking to it. I really don't think my mom understood what was going on. She didn't understand that I wouldn't be around for a while. She had no concept of moving away and she had no idea where Alabama was located. She didn't seem to realize how far Alabama was from Delaware. She didn't understand that I wouldn't be able to just get in my car and drive over to her house anymore. Just when I thought she got it, she would say or ask me something that made me realize that she didn't get it at all. I knew that she was confused and I didn't expect her to understand. The good thing about her not understanding was that she didn't seem to be sad. She wasn't upset that we were leaving and I never saw her shed one single tear over it. If she had been upset about it, I don't know what I would have done. It would have definitely made it much harder for me to leave. For once, I was glad that she was blissfully unaware of what was going on. It made it that much easier to actually leave.

A few days before we left, we had a going away party with our families at my parents' house. It gave us a chance to see everyone one last time before we left. I remember feeling like everyone was probably judging me for my decision to leave. I felt like they all couldn't believe that I was actually going to do it. I had talked about it for so long and now it was finally about to happen. I wondered if everyone thought that there was a chance that I wouldn't go through with it. I felt like everyone thought I was being selfish because I was leaving my dad with no one to help. I thought that they all felt like I was abandoning him. "How can she just up and leave him like that?" "Who's going to help out while she's gone?" "What if her mom forgets who she is while she's away?" "How can she do that to them? She is being so selfish!" It didn't matter that no one actually said any of these things to me. I had convinced myself that it was what they were all thinking. I mean, it was what *I* was thinking most of the time, so how could they not be thinking it, too?

At the end of the party, everyone said their goodbyes and wished us good luck. Just a few days later, we loaded up our cars and a U-Haul with all of our stuff. We were leaving our house practically empty and vacant. My parents came over with coffee and breakfast sandwiches on the morning of our departure. It took all of the strength I had inside of me not to cry. I knew that if I cried, then my mom would get upset and probably start crying, too. I would never be able to leave her that way. So, I choked back tears and tried to stay positive. I knew that I could talk to them as much as I wanted while I was gone and I had planned on coming home to visit every two months. As soon as we left, I could begin counting down the days until my first visit. It was time for us to go. It was time for us to embark on a new adventure and begin a new chapter in our lives together. Everything was going to be fine. Everything would work out. That's what I kept telling myself. I put on my big girl pants, hugged and kissed my parents goodbye, and, just like that, we were off.

We broke our trip up into three days, stopping twice to stay at a hotel for the night. The drive to Alabama went very smoothly. We didn't run into any issues and there was hardly any traffic. We arrived to Fort Rucker on a Friday morning and went to the housing office to get the keys to our house. A woman from the office had us follow her over to the house they had assigned us. I didn't know what to expect, but when we got to the house, I was relieved. The house was in a location that I thought was absolutely perfect. It was as if I had chosen it myself. There were no houses on either side or across the street from our house. We had plenty of space and privacy. When we walked into the house, I was even more relieved. It was beautiful and I could tell that it had been recently updated. The cabinets, countertops, carpeting, and hardwood floors all looked brand new. The house wasn't too big or too small. It was just right. Perfect for us. Even Oakley seemed to approve of the house, as he pooped in the backyard within minutes of our arrival. My husband had to go back over to the housing office to sign some paperwork, so Oakley and I stayed at the house by ourselves. I went out into the backyard with him to look around. I took a nice, deep breath and exhaled. We were home. I had a feeling that it was going to be a good year.

Once my husband got back, we spent the rest of the day unloading the U-Haul. We didn't really know anyone well enough to ask for help, so it was just the two of us. We unloaded both of our cars and the U-Haul all by ourselves. Beds, couches, tables, dressers, and box after box after box. I kept reminding my husband how lucky he was that he had a strong wife. That I wasn't one of those girly, prissy women, who was too good to lift a finger to help out. We had almost everything unloaded by the end of the day and had already started to unpack the essentials. We were both very excited to begin this new chapter in our lives. It felt amazing to be in a new environment with new surroundings. A fresh start. Once we started to unpack and get settled in, it really started to feel like home. Sweet Home Alabama.

As our first few days in Alabama passed, we were able to finish unpacking and settling into our new house and our new lives. My husband started work on the Monday after we had arrived. I was beginning my role as an Army wife. Although I had not been working for over a year by the time we moved to Fort Rucker, I had been constantly busy helping out with my mom. Now, for the first time in a long time, I felt like I had a lot of free time. I honestly didn't know what I was going to do with myself for the next year, but I thought I would just enjoy taking a break for a while. I went to the gym or ran every morning and took Oakley for plenty of walks. I was surprised by all of the people that I saw out and about in the neighborhood in the middle of the day. It dawned on me that for the first time ever I was living in a neighborhood where a majority of the women didn't work. Everyone was home all day with their kids. I wasn't the only one who didn't have a job. No one here was going to judge me for not working. Once I realized that, I began to relax. It took a lot of the pressure off of me to figure out what I wanted to do with my life. It was ok that I didn't know what I wanted to do. It was ok to do nothing for a while. I figured that all of this down time would give me an opportunity to think about what I really wanted to do and, hopefully, I would have it figured out by the time we moved back to Delaware. I wanted to go home with a plan.

I started to really enjoy my down time and began to do something that I hadn't done in a long time. Socialize. After five years in law enforcement, ending two ten-year-long friendships, and over a year of taking care of my mom, I had become pretty anti-social. I was over people. I didn't want to hang out with the people that I already knew and I sure as shit didn't want to meet any new ones. Everyone would always be like, "Oh, I just love meeting new people," and I'd be like, "Nah, I'm good." I didn't want anything to do with anyone. I didn't trust anyone. I just wanted to be left alone. However, moving to Fort Rucker, I had told myself that I was going to have to be more social. This was a place where I didn't know anyone except for my husband, who would be gone all the time. Unless I wanted to sit at home alone for the next year, I was going to have to make some friends.

I was a little nervous about this venture because I didn't think I was going to have anything in common with anyone. For one thing, it seemed as though everyone had at least one kid. I didn't have any kids and I didn't want any kids. Ever. I didn't even really like kids all that much. Well, some are ok, but I just didn't like kids in general. I was also worried because I don't like a lot of things that most girls like. I hate cooking, crafting, makeup, painting my nails, or wearing anything besides gym clothes. I hate country music. I've never seen or read any of that Twilight or Hunger Games crap. And Zumba is not my idea of a workout. I just wanted to run, lift weights, play with my dog, and eat pizza. I was not about to join any book clubs or crafting groups. I decided that I was just going to be myself and if no one liked me, then they could all just fuck off.

I was surprised at how easy it was to make friends at Fort Rucker. I was honestly baffled by the number of women who saw me walking Oakley and stopped me to introduce themselves. That was something that I would never do. One neighbor offered to make us a meal and bring it over to our house. I remember thinking, "Why?!" I came from a place where if someone offered to make me something to eat, I would graciously accept it and then throw it in the trash as soon as they left. My first thought would have been that someone was trying to poison the two cops that lived in the neighborhood. Ummm, no, thank you! It just didn't feel natural to me to walk around the neighborhood smiling, introducing myself to everyone, and handing out apple pies. That just wasn't me. I realized that I could still be me while allowing other people to be themselves, too. We didn't have to all be exactly alike in order to be friends. I began to step outside of my comfort zone by accepting invitations and inviting other women to do things. I went to parties, coffee dates, lunch dates, and girls' nights. I met a bunch of different girls and instantly clicked with a few of them. Before I knew it, I had made a few new friends.

I think the best part was that I was truly being myself. I didn't have to change who I was in order for people to like me. I don't have a fake bone in my body. It crushes my soul to have to pretend to be someone I'm not. But, I felt that I had been pretending for a long time. Somewhere between working in law enforcement, caring for my mom, and struggling to keep dying friendships alive, I had lost myself. I forgot who I was. I forgot what mattered to me and what didn't, what was important to me and what wasn't. I forgot what I liked and disliked, what I believed in and what I didn't. I forgot what my strengths and weaknesses were. I forgot what I stood for and what I was passionate about. I forgot what made me, me. I forgot how it felt to not have to make an effort to just be myself. To not have to smile and fake it, but to truly be happy. I forgot how it felt to put myself out there and not care what anyone thought. I forgot how it felt to laugh, not because I thought I should, but because something was actually funny. For the first time in years, I was finding myself again and I felt completely comfortable just being me.

After just a couple of months in Alabama, I became a mother of two. We decided to adopt another black lab, a female, named Lucy. Lucy is a real silly goose. She is wild and crazy, but even more sweet and loving. Lucy is a fierce protector and a loyal companion. She loves her brother, Oakley, and he loves her, too, even though she gets on his nerves sometimes. The two of them play and snuggle together like they have always been brother and sister. They absolutely melt my heart. I love my little pack more than anything and am proud to call myself a crazy dog mom. The best part of being a mother of two is that I now have an endless supply of crazy stories to tell my mom about Oakley and Lucy. My mom loves to hear all about them. She might not be able to follow along with most of the things I tell her, but she can always follow along with stories about Oakley and Lucy. On days when I am struggling to keep a conversation going with her, I usually end up talking about Oakley and Lucy. I can almost always think of a new story to tell my mom and she loves every minute of it. Becoming a mother of two was quite an adjustment, but it has made my life that much better and more fulfilling. I love being a mommy to my two crazy pooches and I openly embrace my inner crazy dog lady.

I knew that living in Alabama was going to be a good experience for me. I knew that it was going to be a year of growth and discovery. I had intended on using my year in Alabama to "find myself." I had a feeling that was exactly what I was going to do. Being in Alabama for just a couple of months had given me a chance to catch my breath. I finally had the time, space, and distance that I had been craving for a while now. I was already starting to feel better about myself and just better in general. I just had to deal with the guilt and difficulty of being so far away from my parents for so long. However, this turned out to be no easy task.

As time went on, life went on. As much as I wanted to think that my mom was the same as when I left her in August, she simply was not. Other people who talked to or saw her regularly might disagree, but, to me, she was different. With me living over 900 miles away from my mom, I relied heavily on our phone conversations to keep in touch with her. I tried to call my mom every two or three days. Our conversations varied in length, but they were about thirty minutes long on average. As time went on, I began finding it harder and harder to have a conversation with my mom. She was becoming a stranger to me. I often felt as though I had nothing to talk to her about. I struggled to come up with things to discuss, but I was always at a loss. There was never any conversation on her end and I knew that if I didn't talk, there would be complete and utter silence.

Making it all the more difficult, this horrible disease continued to cloud her mind and steal it away from all of us. I couldn't ask my mom what she had been up to or what she did over the weekend. She wouldn't be able to tell me because she wouldn't remember. I often asked her questions to which she responded with silence. She was just utterly lost and confused. She was unable to answer me. I didn't know if she didn't understand the question, didn't know the answer, or both. A simple question like, "What did you do today?" was often followed by a long pause. I usually ended up trying to guess what she did and she either agreed or disagreed. There was no way of ever knowing what she actually did, unless I asked my dad. Having nothing new to discuss on my end, our conversations always ended up sounding like a broken record. My mom asked me the same few questions repeatedly and told me the same few things over and over again. It reminded me of making small talk with someone in line at the grocery store. It felt like we didn't even know each other. Like we were complete strangers.

In many ways, we *were* strangers. My mom had no idea what state I was living in. When I said Alabama, she feigned recollection, but I honestly doubted that she even had a clue. She would ask me what I was doing and I told her that I was just hanging around the house. She would ask me what house and where it was. She always asked me when I was coming home to Delaware, which was like a knife in my heart every single time. She always asked me about my husband and my dogs, Oakley and Lucy. Although she always remembered to ask how they were, she didn't always remember their names. Or, she remembered the name Steve Dykovitz, but she forgot how I was related to him or that he was my husband. Most of the time, she didn't even remember my last name. Oddly enough, she seemed to remember Lucy's name the best and Lucy had only been in the family for a few short months. She always said, "Lucy! I just love that name. Like the show, 'I Love Lucy.'" Now, how the hell could she remember that was a TV show, but she couldn't remember where I was or why I was there? It made no fucking sense.

She didn't understand the concept that we were living in Alabama while Steve went to flight school. She only sometimes remembered that was the whole reason we were in Alabama in the first place. She always asked me what Steve was doing. She dreaded him going into the military, but she didn't understand that he was already in the military. Yet, she was the most patriotic person I knew and probably one of the proudest of Steve. She also forgot that he was a police officer back at home and that I used to be one, as well. She always asked me how I became a police officer and what kind of training I needed. She forgot that I lived with her during the police academy and that she attended my graduation. She forgot that I went to college. How fucking sad is it that she had lost all of those memories? Memories of her children's accomplishments. Memories of what they were doing now. Memories of her loved one's names and where they lived. Memories of a question that she asked at least 57 times and would continue to ask because she forgot that she already asked it those 57 times. My mom didn't know or remember a thing about me or my life. She didn't remember my past and she forgot my present. Or, she just didn't understand it.

My mom didn't understand the whole military life and living on a military base. She always asked me how I was able to call home and how much it cost, as if she thought I was in prison or something. She also always asked me if I was allowed to do things, like have visitors. I guess I couldn't fault her too much for not understanding since she didn't have much experience with the military life, but, still, most people would have understood. She often asked me if I had seen Steve lately. It was like she didn't know that we lived together and I saw him every single day, if even just for a few minutes. Although she was very proud of Steve, she had no clue what he was doing. She was just simply unable to understand. She couldn't even remember the word "helicopter" or how to pronounce it.

Aside from not remembering most things, my mom was becoming increasingly confused and disoriented. She didn't know where she was, where I was, or the relation between those two places. Often times when I called my mom, she couldn't tell me where she was. She would say that she was at her house, but she was actually at my aunt's house. Or vice versa. I would ask her if my dad was home and she would say that he was, but he was actually at work. Or, she said that he was at work, but he was actually in the other room. One time, I called my mom and she asked me, "How are your mom and dad?" Then, she quickly caught herself and tried to make a joke out of it. Another time, I called my mom and she said that she was watching TV with my sister, who I knew would have been at work at the time. Then, I heard her asking, "Who's here? Who's here?" It turns out that my Aunt Diane and Nan were actually the ones watching TV with her. Most of the time she had no idea where she was or who she was with.

In addition, she wasn't able to distinguish between talking to someone on the phone and seeing them in person. On a few occasions, when I called her, she asked me, "When did you get here?" or "How did you get here?" It was as if she thought I was standing right in front of her instead of being on the other end of the phone. I explained to her that I wasn't there, but that I was on the phone with her. Then, we would go through the whole ordeal of me explaining that I was at my house in Alabama because we were living down there while Steve went to flight school. She often mentioned having seen people that I knew she had only talked to on the phone. Or, she would say that someone had called her when they actually came to her house or she had seen them somewhere. During one visit home, she was sitting in the living room downstairs, while I was upstairs getting showered and dressed. I yelled down to her to make sure that she was ok and that she didn't need anything. As I was talking to her, I heard her pick up her cell phone. I knew that she was talking into her cell phone, thinking that I was on the phone instead of upstairs. She even asked me when I was coming over to pick her up. When we were finished talking, she said, "Ok, I'll talk to you later," and I heard her hang up her cell phone. She forgot people, places, things, facts, concepts, and the relationship between it all. She forgot pretty much everything.

Needless to say, it had become increasingly, extremely difficult to have a conversation on the phone with her. I would have loved to have seen her more often, but, in between visits, the phone was all we had and it quickly became nothing at all. My mom quickly became a stranger to me. Although she still knew who I was, she didn't know anything about me. And, I often felt like I didn't know anything about her either. Obviously, I love my mom very much, which makes this hard to say, but, sometimes, when I looked into her eyes, I felt nothing. Her eyes looked through me, past me, but not *at* me. I didn't know her anymore. I knew that this was all part of the disease and I knew that this would happen, but it didn't make it any easier. I missed my mom every day. And, not just in the sense that we were apart from each other. I would have missed my mom even if I was sitting right next to her and looking into her distant eyes. She was in there, somewhere, but she was buried deep beneath the surface and sometimes the Alzheimer's was all I could see. When I looked at her, sometimes a stranger was all I could see. When I talked to her, I barely recognized her voice. Where the fuck did my mom go? She wasn't dead, but it felt like she had died long ago. Her body was still alive, but her mind was not. Her mind had been stolen, stripped away, and replaced with the mind of stranger. A stranger who was more like a confused, disoriented, and scared little girl than anyone's wife or mother. I knew that the mother who raised me was somewhere deep inside of this stranger who had replaced her. And, I was still desperate to have as much of a relationship with her as I possibly could.

I continued calling my mom every two or three days, sometimes more. I was constantly worried about what was going on that I wasn't there to see. I could only imagine that it was much worse than I even knew. I mean, what I knew was bad enough and I only talked to her every few days and saw her every two months. Each time I went home to visit my parents, my mom's condition was worse. I saw things that I couldn't see when I talked to her on the phone. She was forgetting how to walk, how to enter doorways, how to go up and down stairs, how to sit in a chair, how to use the bathroom, and the list goes on and on. These were things that I would never know just from talking to her on the phone. I couldn't ask her what she did or didn't know how to do. And, asking my dad had never really been an option because he didn't like to talk about it, or anything for that matter.

I have to admit that, at times, I was happy to be away from it all. Although I feel incredibly selfish for admitting it, it was a nice break for me. I could escape from the world of Alzheimer's for a while. I didn't have to see it right in front of my face, all day, every day. It wasn't being shoved down my throat to the point where it was hard for me to breathe. I could breathe. I could pretend that it wasn't there. It was always easier just not to think about it.

This worked sometimes. But, most of the time, I was feeling guilty for leaving and selfish for being able to get away from it all. My dad never got a break from it. He had to deal with it 24 hours a day, 7 days a week. I knew that he wasn't handling it well. He was still very much in denial of my mom's worsening condition and he didn't know how to handle it. He was overwhelmed, stressed out, miserable, and depressed. He was hopeless and it seemed like he had given up. There was nothing that could take away my mom's Alzheimer's, so it seemed as though he didn't see the point in even trying to make anything better. I felt like it was all my fault. When I lived near them, I was able to go over to their house a few times a week to help out and give my dad a break. When I moved, I abandoned him. I left him alone to deal with it all. The year and five months that I lived away was that much harder for him because I wasn't there to help out. I could stop thinking about it for as long as I wanted, but it was always there waiting for me. When I did start thinking about it, I always felt the same. Like shit.

When we moved to Alabama, I told myself that I was going to try to go home every two months so that I could see my mom. I was afraid that she was going to forget who I was while we were living away. I wanted her to see my face as much as possible so that she wouldn't forget me. The reality was that she was going to forget me one day no matter how many times she saw me. When I started making my trips home, I quickly learned that it didn't really matter all that much for my mom to see me every two months. It mattered much more for my dad. He needed me home much more than she did. I tried to help him out as much as I could while I was home. I wanted to give him as much of a break as I possibly could. I knew that my mom was always happy to see me, but I realized that my dad was the one who *needed* to see me.

My visits at home were a lot of work. They were never really enjoyable. I always hated it when I got back to Alabama and someone would ask me if I had a good trip home. The short answer was, "Yes," but that was a complete lie. I knew that no one really wanted to hear me go on and on about how stressful and emotional my trip home had been. No one really wanted to hear the truth, so I always lied. The truth was that each trip home was an emotional shit-storm. It always took me at least a few days to recover once I got back to Alabama. I don't think that anyone really understood what these trips were like. I wasn't sleeping in and having chocolate chip pancakes in bed while my mom braided my hair. We weren't reminiscing and flipping through old photo albums. It didn't feel like

I was back in high school again. I was stressed-the-fuck-out from the minute I left my house in Alabama to the minute I got back.

First of all, I have major, crazy-ass, mental-patient, should-probably-be-on-meds-but-I'm-not OCD. The laundry, the packing, the unpacking, the repacking, the unpacking again, and the laundry again routine was enough to make me the next *Girl, Interrupted.* It drove me insane. No matter how many trips I took or suitcases I packed, it always stressed me out beyond belief. Not to mention the fact that I always came home to a house that my husband had been living in freely, without restrictions, for a whole week. It always took me at least two days to do my laundry, pack, and get everything in order to leave for my trip. I tried to take care of everything before I left so that my husband didn't have to worry about anything while I was gone. He could just focus on flying and studying. Then, it took me at least another two days to get my house back in order (to my OCD standards), unpack, do my laundry, and decompress when I got back from my trip. Yeah, I know, I'm crazy. I'm always the first one to admit it. I own my craziness, so y'all don't have to talk about me behind my back. I'm the 2007 version of my girl Britney Spears, except it's 2016 and there will be no comeback for me.

Aside from my OCD struggles, there were other factors that contributed to the stress. My trips home were always an emotional fucking rollercoaster. Staying at your parents' house for a week as an adult is one thing, but staying at their house for a week when your mom has Alzheimer's is quite another. I don't know if the average person knew what these trips home were like for me. I mean, some people probably thought that going home to visit my parents was like an episode of *7th Heaven*. It wasn't. My mom didn't clean my room, fluff my pillows, or make me breakfast, lunch, and dinner every day. She never made me my favorite home-cooked meal or took me shopping for new clothes. We didn't play board games together or paint each other's nails. I didn't go home so that my mom could pamper me and take care of me. It was exactly the opposite. I went home to take care of her. She needed help with basically everything at that point. And so, my trips home usually went a little something like this.

I arrived at the Philadelphia Airport, headed to baggage claim, and stepped outside to meet my parents, who always picked me up. Without fail, a big, huge wave of depression and sadness hit me like a bus. You would think that I would have been excited to see them. I *was* excited to see them, but I never knew what to expect. In between trips, I called my mom every couple of days, but that was totally different than being right there, in front of her. I never knew if her condition was going to be noticeably worse or if she was having a good day or a bad one. I never knew how hard it had been on my dad that day or what kind of mood he was going to be in. I never made plans with anyone for the first or second day that I was home because I wanted to spend time with my mom and dad. For some reason, knowing that I was going to be spending the next 48 hours with them made me feel like I was stuck and suffocating. Harsh, but true. Sure, I could have easily made plans with friends for the first or second day that I was home, but I didn't want it to feel like I was running off the minute I got off the plane. So, I just dealt with it. I let the wave of depression and sadness hit me and I submerged myself in it. I let it surround me and wash over my head, for I knew, like all waves, that this would pass.

Once the depression faded and we arrived at my parents' house, I endured the stress of unpacking my suitcase. While I knew that I didn't necessarily have to unpack, I liked to do it anyway. My parents' house had become one hell of a disorganized and cluttered mess since my mom got Alzheimer's. Unpacking my bag, putting my clothes in the drawers and hanging them in the closet, and lining my shoes up neatly in a row, allowed me to feel some sense of control and organization. Once everything was in its place, it calmed me. I immediately felt more settled in and more relaxed. Although the process of unpacking was stressful to me, I knew that it would be worth it once I was done. After I unpacked, I usually made a trip to ShopRite to load up on the essentials for the next week. My parents had hardly any food in their house and a lot of it was stuff that I didn't eat anyway, so I always made a trip to the store myself. Plus, anyone who knows me knows that ShopRite donuts are my drug of choice. They were a must for my first night home, along with my favorite pizza from Marino's. Feeling fat and happy after eating all of my favorite junk foods, I always started to feel better. But, I knew that the feeling wouldn't last long because each trip was filled with many high and lows.

The highs were getting my hair cut and colored along with my mom, having dinner with all of my homegirls, and the tradition of breakfast and shopping with my bestie. The highs were taking my mom to the park, making her laugh, and hearing her say that she never wants to leave. The highs were quizzing her on her ABC's, 123's, and spelling and seeing how proud she was when she got the answers right. The highs were when my mom let me help her change into her pajamas and tuck her into bed at night, and when she helped me do the laundry and clean the house. She was always so proud of herself for being able to help out and contribute. The highs were when she raved about the PB&J that I made her for lunch or when I was able to get her to eat something for breakfast, even though my dad couldn't. The highs were watching *Homeward Bound* and *Marley & Me* with her and dancing to Elvis. The highs were when she was laughing and I knew that she was happy. The highs were when she was present, in the moment, fully knowing who I was, who she is, and how we are related to each other. Nothing was better than having a real conversation with my mom. It didn't happen often, but, when it did, it was pure happiness.

Of course, with all of the highs came just as many lows, if not more. The lows were not being able to have a real conversation with my mom because she didn't understand what the hell I was talking about. The lows were when she forgot who I was, who she was, and how we are related to each other. We could spend the whole day together, but if we were apart for more than five minutes, she could completely forget who I was or how I got there. The lows were when my mom didn't know her sister's name or who she was, even though we were sitting right next to her and had been with her all day. The lows were having to hold my mom's hand and lead her to the bathroom, the back porch, or her bedroom in her own house every time she wanted to go somewhere. The lows were when my mom said she wanted to go sit on the back porch with my dad, so I took her there, but once we got there, she was too cold and wanted to go back inside. Then, when she was back inside and sat in the living room again, she said that she wanted to go sit on the porch with my dad. I took her to the porch every single time, even though I knew that she would be too cold and I would be leading her right back inside again. The lows were having to cut her pizza, sandwich, or other food into small pieces so that she would be able to eat it. The lows were listening to my mom give my dad a hard time because he hadn't been spending any time with her, even though he'd been with her all day. The lows were when my mom cried and said that she was tired of being alone all the time because she didn't realize that my dad or I had been with her all day. The lows were looking at my dad and seeing sadness, depression, loneliness, and desperation in his eyes. The lows were listening to my dad whining, begging, and pleading with my mom to try to get her to do something as simple as walk into another room. The lows were watching my mom struggle to find her words, the refrigerator, the bathroom, or a chair. The lows were when we were walking back to the car after having a nice morning at the park and a stranger said hello to us, but my mom was convinced that the stranger was her mom. She didn't understand how her mom got there or why she was there. Even after trying to convince her otherwise, she still thought that this stranger was her mom and she wouldn't let it go. The lows were having to take care of my mom as if she were my child instead. The lows were realizing that she could no longer do yet another thing that she was once able to do and knowing that her condition was getting worse. But, by far, the worst of the lows was when she knew that something was wrong with her and she became embarrassed or apologetic over something that she did. That was like the sharpest knife in the world stabbing me right in my fucking heart. The pain was unbearable.

Looking at this list, there seemed to be many more lows than there were highs. When the lows hit, it was really low, but when the highs came around, it was *so high*. Nothing made me feel better than the sound of my mom's laughter and the smile on her face. She lit up like a little girl on Christmas. Still, there were multiple times during my trips when I called or texted my husband and said things like, "I'm so fucking over this," "I'm ready to come home," "I can't take this anymore," or "Fucking kill me." Even though I could be overwhelmed at times, I was always sad to head back to the airport and leave my parents. I knew that I would miss them and I was sad that I wouldn't be there to help out for a while. I worried about them all the time. I usually broke down crying at some point during my first or second day back in Alabama. Like I said before, each trip home was an emotional rollercoaster.

I could have easily stayed at my own house back in Delaware whenever I went home to visit, but I chose not to. My house was all closed up and practically empty inside, plus there was no cable or Wi-Fi. I chose to stay with my parents so that I could be there 24/7 to help out and to give my dad a break. My trips home were not meant to be a vacation or a break for me. My trips home were not about *me*. They were about *her*. They were about *him*. The two people who gave me life, raised me, and had always taken care of me. Now it was my turn to give back and I truly wouldn't have had it any other way.

As my year in Alabama went on, I continued to call my mom every couple of days and go home to visit her every couple of months. Some people might think that it was easier for me to be away from my mom than it would have been for me to be there taking care of her. To a point, I would have to agree. However, nothing about being 900 miles away from her was easy. Not one single day went by that I didn't think about her multiple times a day. I was usually consumed with guilt, worry, and sadness. I knew that the time I spent away from her was precious time that I could have been spending with her. It was very difficult for me to give up that time. It was very difficult to uproot my life to move away from the people that I loved most in the world. I wished that I could have been in two places at once. That would have been the only way that I would have felt complete and settled. Although it was never easy being away from my mom, I was determined to make my time away count. I was determined to use that time to do something that my mom would be proud of. And, I was determined more than ever to find my purpose and to start living it.

A Purpose, Not a Paycheck

Ever since I can remember, I have always loved to write. My favorite class in school was English. I actually thought that it was fun to diagram sentences in middle school. I never complained about having to write short stories, essays, or even research papers. I was a Communications Arts major at my high school, Cab Calloway School of the Arts. I always thought that I would major in Journalism in college, but I decided to major in Criminal Justice instead to pursue a career as a lawyer. At some point during college, I reverted back to my childhood dream of being a police officer. But, as you all know by now, that plan didn't turn out so well. Even though I hated being a police officer, I never really minded writing reports or warrants. And, anyone who's ever read any of my police reports could tell you that I could write one hell of a police report. I think everyone would agree on that.

After my stint in law enforcement came to an end, I had absolutely no idea what I wanted to do with my life. If someone had asked me what my dream job would have been, I would have said that I wanted to be a writer. However, I had convinced myself that being a writer was not realistic and that it certainly wasn't going to make me any money. Still, writing had always been my passion. It was something that I truly loved to do. People were always telling me that if you do something you love, you will never work a day in your life. I knew that if writing was my job, it would never feel like work to me. But, how would I even begin a career as a writer? What would I even write about?

As my mom's Alzheimer's progressed and I gained more experience in dealing with it, I had always considered the idea of starting a blog to share my story. Writing about my experiences would be very therapeutic for me and it would allow me to sort through my feelings about my mom's Alzheimer's. I also thought that sharing my story about Alzheimer's might help other people who were going through the same thing. Other people might be able to relate to what I wrote and it would remind them that they were not alone. I really wasn't even sure how to start writing a blog or how to begin telling my story. Plus, I was living close to my parents and helping take care of my mom, so I never really had the time to sit down and write. It was something that I had always wanted to do, but I just never really found the time.

Well, less than two months after moving to Alabama, I finally found the time. It was October 2014 and I had just returned to Alabama from my first visit back home to see my parents. I was full of conflicting emotions and never-ending thoughts. As I mentioned earlier on, I am not the type of person to call my friends and just start complaining about my problems. I know that everyone has their own shit to deal with and I didn't want to bother anyone with my shit. I didn't want to be that annoying person who only called her friends when she had something to whine and complain about. Still, I definitely needed an outlet for my thoughts and feelings. I remembered my idea to start a blog. Writing a blog would be the perfect outlet for me. I could feel free to go on and on for as long as I wanted. If someone didn't want to hear about it, then they didn't have to read my blog. Even if no one ever read any of my blog posts, I would still be able to get my thoughts and feelings out so that I could begin to work through them. However, I have some pretty awesome and supportive friends and family, who have always loved my writing, so I had a feeling that people would be reading it. I knew that there would never be a better time to start.

I really only knew of two blog sites so I just picked one, created a login and password, and just like that, I started a blog. I decided to start with a welcome post to tell everyone about my blog, what it would be about, and why I was writing it. I shared the link on my Facebook page and the reaction was amazing. Everyone was very supportive and excited to start reading my blog posts. Everyone thought writing a blog was a great idea and that it would be a great outlet for me. A lot of people told me that I was brave and courageous for sharing my story. I have to say, I have never considered myself to be brave or courageous for sharing my story. I am pretty much an open book. If you ask me, I'll tell you. I try to tell it like it is and to be as real as possible. The thought of putting myself out there and making myself vulnerable had never occurred to me. It was never a factor in my decision to start publicly sharing my story with others. I liked my privacy just as much as the next guy, but, to me, my story wasn't private. It wasn't meant to be locked away somewhere for no one to ever hear it. It was meant to be told and shared with everyone, everywhere. It was meant to help others whose stories sounded a lot like mine. It was meant to help educate others who had never heard a story like mine. It was meant to make people laugh and cry and, most importantly, think. It was meant to raise awareness about a pretty fucked up disease called Alzheimer's. A storm like no other. It was meant to help others weather their own storms.

As soon as I started writing my blog, I knew that it was the right thing to do. I always shared my new blog posts on my Facebook page and everyone was very supportive. People told me that they loved reading my posts. They loved hearing my story and they loved the way that I told it. Of course, these people were mostly my friends, family, and acquaintances. Although I greatly appreciated their kind words, most of them had never dealt with Alzheimer's personally, so they couldn't really relate to my story. However, there were a few people on my friends list, who I really didn't know at all, who reached out to me and told me about their connection to Alzheimer's. There were two women in particular, who I knew from working at the police department, who had both lost their mother to Alzheimer's. I didn't know that and probably never would have known that if I hadn't started my blog. I was amazed at the connection and bond that I formed with these two ladies simply because we shared a story. These two women always told me how much they loved my blog and how much they could relate to what I wrote. That meant the world to me. That meant that I had gotten it right.

I wanted to reach more people who shared my story. I decided to start sharing my blog posts on a couple of Facebook support groups that I had joined. Again, I was amazed at the response. So many people told me that they felt like they had written my post themselves. They had been through or were going through the exact same thing. Everyone told me how much they loved my writing and the way I told my story. They liked that I didn't sugarcoat anything or leave anything out. They could all relate to my thoughts, feelings, and experiences. It meant so much to me that people who shared my experiences were able to relate to my blog posts. It meant that I was getting it right. It was my story to tell, but I had always wanted to make sure that I was telling it in a way that made it sound familiar to others who had been through it. The responses from people who had experience with Alzheimer's proved to me that I was.

I continued to write my blog and share the posts with as many people as I could. I also began to share more personal stories, pictures, videos, and information about Alzheimer's on my Facebook page. I had always shared these things, but I started to do it much more often than I had before. I didn't even care if anyone "liked" or "commented" on anything. It was just something that I liked to do for myself. Over time, I started receiving private messages on Facebook from people who wanted to share a link or a video about Alzheimer's that they thought I might like. I truly appreciated these messages because it meant that people were paying attention to me. It meant that my story wasn't falling on deaf ears. People were listening and taking an interest when they otherwise might not have. I felt that my story put a face to Alzheimer's for these people. They might not have ever known anyone else that had dealt with Alzheimer's, especially someone my age or my mom's age. But now, they had seen my pictures, videos, and posts. Now when they heard something about Alzheimer's, they thought of me. And, that meant something.

I also began to receive private messages from people who were seeking advice about Alzheimer's. I received messages from several different people who told me that someone they knew had begun showing signs of Alzheimer's or had just been diagnosed with it. These people were looking for advice on the symptoms, how to get their loved ones diagnosed, or what doctors to go to. They were looking for advice on what to do after they received a diagnosis, where to begin, or what medications their loved ones should be taking. They wanted to know how my family and I had handled certain situations with my mom. But, I think that they mostly wanted to know someone else who had been through it. They wanted to know that they were not alone in this fight. And, when they were trying to think of someone they knew who had been there, they thought of me.

After years of beating myself over the head trying to determine my purpose, it seemed that I had finally found it. I realized that there is a big difference between having a paycheck and having a purpose. A paycheck is necessary to survive. It pays the bills, puts food on the table, and puts a roof over your head. A paycheck makes you feel like you are contributing to your household. It makes you feel useful. But, a paycheck does not necessarily give you a purpose. A purpose is the reason you wake up each day. It gives you motivation, drive, and a sense of worth. It makes you feel needed. Fulfilling your purpose is something that you would probably do for free because you cannot put a monetary value on how it makes you feel inside. A paycheck says a lot about what you do, but a purpose says a lot about who you are.

When you have a purpose, you know it. You can feel it. You live and breathe it. A purpose means owning everything in purple because it is the Alzheimer's awareness color, even though I never really liked purple all that much. Though I have to say, it has grown on me. A purpose means reading, watching, and listening to everything that has anything to do with Alzheimer's. A purpose means telling anyone who will listen about Alzheimer's and sharing your story with them. A purpose means feeling fulfilled by what you do even if you're not earning a paycheck from doing it. Maybe I will earn a paycheck by fulfilling my purpose someday, but, even if I don't, I will still do it. You can't place a monetary value on how something makes you feel inside. You can't pay for happiness and fulfillment. Nothing makes me feel happier or more fulfilled than knowing that my words have touched someone else's life. That my words were seen by the eyes or heard by the ears of someone who really needed them. I know that there must be someone out there reading this that feels just as sad, dark, and alone as I once felt. I want my words to wrap around her, squeeze her tight, and whisper, "You are not alone." If sharing my story can help even one person, then it's worth it.

Well, now that I had found my purpose, I wanted to find more ways to fulfill it. I was already writing a blog and using my personal Facebook page to promote Alzheimer's awareness, but I wanted to do more. A couple of years ago, I had the idea of starting a non-profit organization called Pawz for Alz. Pawz for Alz would involve people volunteering to visit Alzheimer's patients with their dogs. The visits would occur in nursing homes or in assisted living homes, but also in the private residences of Alzheimer's patients and their caregivers. These visits would provide pet therapy to the patients, as well as to their caregivers. My parents were the inspiration for this idea. They are both major dog-lovers and they benefit greatly from time spent with their grand-dogs, Oakley and

Lucy. I would do absolutely anything to bring a smile to either one of their faces, especially my dad. He loves spending time with Oakley and Lucy whenever I bring them over to his house. Often times, he will come to my house to pick them up and take them for a nice, long walk somewhere. He really enjoys spending time with them. My mom also loves them both to death. She loves to watch Oakley swim in their pool and she loves to snuggle with Lucy. Oakley and Lucy have even had several sleepovers at my mom and dad's house. My dad always tells me how they all cuddle up in bed together at night. My mom and dad just love it.

There are days that my mom can't remember my name, but she never ever forgets Oakley's or Lucy's name. And, the best part about doggie therapy is that even if my mom did forget Lucy's name, Lucy would never even know. She would never be upset or offended by it. She would never judge my mom for it or for anything else, such as wearing her shirt inside out or backwards. She would never judge my mom for saying something strange or for the fact that she hasn't washed her hair in weeks. She would never judge her for not being able to effectively participate in a conversation. Dogs are incapable of judging people or being rude to them. They can't give someone a dirty look. They are incapable of being impatient with people or verbally snapping at them. They don't exclude anyone for being different or not fitting in. Dogs are only capable of loving people. If you love him and treat him well, a dog will be your best friend and your companion for life. They make the most loyal friends and they will always look out for you. They will always be there for you. Who better to have by your side when battling such a horrific disease as Alzheimer's? A dog will never let you down. He will never leave your side. He will never talk about you behind your back. All he will do is love you.

So, Pawz for Alz would have volunteers take their dogs for weekly or monthly visits with Alzheimer's patients and their caregivers, to provide some joy and some relief to them through doggie therapy. The patients and caregivers can pet and snuggle with the dogs. They can feed them treats or take them for walks, if they are able to do so. Or, they can just sit back and watch the dogs play fetch or do tricks. The visits would be on a case by case basis so that they can be tailored to meet the needs of each individual patient. We would do whatever it takes to bring a smile to the patient and caregiver's faces. Obviously, the dogs and their handlers would have to be certified at some point. And, there are a lot of logistics and details that would need to be worked out before this idea came to fruition. But, every big idea has to start somewhere small, right?

My first small step toward this big idea was creating a team for The Longest Day fundraiser for the Alzheimer's Association. Each team is tasked with participating in an activity that they love throughout the day on the summer solstice, which is the longest day of the year. Each team also raises money for the Alzheimer's Association. My team, Pawz for Alz, participated in dog-related activities throughout the day. Team members walked their dogs, played with them, took them to the dog park, or did other activities that they enjoy doing with their pooches. I also decided to contact a few local assisted living homes so that I could bring the much calmer of my two dogs, Oakley, in to visit with the Alzheimer's residents. I wanted to do this as part of my fundraiser, but also just in general. Like I said, it was my small first step toward my much bigger and long-term goal of starting a non-profit organization. I was extremely thrilled and thankful when I heard back from one of the facilities, The Terrace at Grove Park, located in Dothan, AL, who said that they would love for me and Oakley to come in for a trial visit. I was told that if the trial visit went well, then we could set up a schedule for future visits. Knowing that Oakley had no professional training and was not a certified therapy dog, I was grateful that this facility was willing to give us a chance anyway.

We had our trial visit on May 26, 2015. Oakley and I arrived a few minutes early so that Oakley could sniff around outside and go potty if he needed to. We were both a little nervous and unsure of what to expect. Oakley was also very excited to be in a new place and to smell all the new smells. The Terrace at Grove Park was an absolutely beautiful community. The main building looked exactly like a southern plantation home. It had a huge front porch, which was lined with white rocking chairs. Oakley and I liked it right away. We walked through the front entrance together and told the woman at the front desk that we had arrived. She introduced us to Sharon, who was the woman that I had been speaking to about our visit. Sharon met Oakley and he gave her a bunch of kisses. She explained to us that there was a group of residents that had gathered for singing in one of the parlor rooms. She thought it would be good for us to sit in on some of the singing and then I could introduce Oakley to everyone. We followed her into the parlor room and stood at the front of the room. Someone was playing the piano and the group of residents was singing songs along with it. We listened for a few minutes and once they were done, Sharon introduced me to the group. Then, I introduced Oakley to the group. I told them a little bit about his background and his life now. I told them where he was from and where he lived now. I told them about his family and his little sister, Lucy. I told them all about how he loved to go for walks, swim, and play with Lucy. Then, I walked Oakley around the room to each person and gave them each a chance to say hello to him. As you can imagine, some of the people shied away from Oakley and were afraid of him. But, many others just absolutely loved him. Oakley is such a sweet, gentle boy that he would sit in front of each person as he/she would pet him and talk sweetly to him. There were a few women in particular who made such a fuss over Oakley and were obviously very excited to see him. Once we finished going around the room, I gave Oakley a few treats to let him know that he did a good job. We gave everyone another chance to see Oakley as they left the room. Oakley and I both felt pretty good about the visit and we knew that we had passed the test. Oakley also felt like he had made out pretty good with all of the attention and treats, especially since he didn't have to share any of it with his little sister.

We followed Sharon into her office and she told us that we passed the trial visit! She said that she would love to have us back again. We decided that Oakley and I would visit once a month from there on out. We scheduled our next visit for the end of June. Sharon and I talked for a few minutes about my mom. She explained to me that not everyone in the group had Alzheimer's. She said that out of the group of 16, probably about 8-10 of them had Alzheimer's. She also said that their Alzheimer's residents were not severe. It struck me that no one in the room seemed to be as far along in the disease as my mom. It also struck me that the group was made up of mostly women, with only one or two men. I explained to Sharon my passion for Alzheimer's awareness and expressed my interest in visiting with the Alzheimer's residents again. Oakley and I were already very excited for our next visit!

On our way out that day, we saw an elderly woman and an elderly man sitting in the rocking chairs on the front porch. The man had on a plaid shirt and jeans that were pulled up way past his belly button. He used a walker to get around and it was clear that he had some difficulties. Oakley went up to the man on his own to say hello. This man spoke so softly and sweetly to Oakley. He kept petting him on the back and rubbing his ears. Oakley was definitely loving it. This man had a smile on his face and a sense of peace in his eyes that made the whole visit worth it. I could tell that he really enjoyed meeting Oakley. I told him that we would be back once a month to visit and he seemed happy with that. Oakley and I walked to the car with our heads held high, knowing that we had done not only a good job, but a good thing. We helped put smiles on a few faces that day. Pawz for Alz may be a long shot. It may just be an idea, a big idea with even bigger goals. But, all of the big things in life are nothing without all of the little things that make them up. The little things like the smile on that man's face that day.

For that reason, we kept going back once a month for the duration of our time in Alabama. We continued to do the same routine as we did during our first visit. I would introduce Oakley to the group and tell them his story. I always told the same story because there were always new people in the group and I knew that some of the people who had met him before would not have remembered it. After I told them all about Oakley, I walked him around the room and gave everyone a chance to love on him. Once we finished saying hello to everyone, I brought Oakley to the center of the room to do the only two tricks he knows. I would have him sit and "give me five." He would slap my hand with his paw and I would give him a treat. Then, I would have him sit and stay while I threw a treat into the air for him to catch. I can proudly say that he caught every single treat and never missed once. Everyone always got a big kick out of Oakley's tricks and would clap for him. Then, I would walk him around the room a second time to give everyone another chance to love on him. We did this same routine on each visit. Oakley and I dressed up as a cowboy and cowgirl for our Halloween visit. For our Christmas visit, which was our last visit, I dressed Oakley up in a Santa outfit and we handed out candy cane reindeer to the residents. They loved it and so did we!

We only made a total of eight visits before we left Alabama, but it was enough for me to know that my dream of Pawz for Alz had a chance at becoming a reality. The smiles on the people's faces when they met Oakley were all I needed. I had begun to recognize the faces of a few people who had been at previous visits with Oakley. Some of them had truly come to love him and I could tell that they were excited when they saw us. There was one woman who appeared to be much younger than everyone else and I learned that she had Alzheimer's. She would hug, kiss, and love on Oakley all day long if I would have let her. She once told me that if I couldn't keep him anymore, then she would take him home with her. There was another woman who was a little bit older and she was nonverbal. Her hands were always balled up and twisted, but she would still pet Oakley the best she could. She would smile at me, nodding her head and moving her lips, but no words would come out. I could tell that she wanted to say something to me, but she could no longer speak. I just smiled back and let her pet Oakley for as long as she wanted. She melted my heart. I may not have known much about the lives of the residents we visited, but I knew that I had given them a few minutes of pure joy. That was enough for me.

Paw for Alz had to be placed on the backburner for a while since we would be leaving Alabama. But, I knew that I would get back to it eventually and that it may even become something bigger than just monthly visits at one assisted living home. So, I had my blog, my awareness posts on my personal Facebook page, my Pawz for Alz visits, and a Pawz for Alz Facebook page to promote our visits and Alzheimer's awareness. What else could I do? How about I write a book?

Everyone who had read and enjoyed my blogs always told me to write a book. I loved the idea, but was terrified of actually doing it. Telling someone to write a book was a lot easier than actually sitting down and writing a book. What if I didn't have enough to write to complete an entire book? What if it never got published and no one ever read it? I decided that I would never know if I never tried. I just sat down one day and started writing. I started at the very beginning of my story and went from there. Three pages turned into ten pages, which turned into fifteen pages, which turned into 40,000 words, and so on. I just decided to keep going until I had nothing left to say and then I would take it from there. Sometimes in life, the destination is not nearly as important as the journey itself. I figured that I would learn a lot about myself by writing everything down. And, if no one ever read it, then at least I would have it to read for myself. I didn't have it all figured out, but that wouldn't stop me from moving forward. The outcome doesn't always necessarily matter. What matters is that you never stop moving forward.

So, that's the story of how this book came to be. Now that I've told you my story up until this point of my life, I would like to share with you some of the things that I've struggled with the most so far along this journey. I would also like to share with you some of the things that I have learned along the way.

Guilt

One thing that I've definitely struggled with the most since my mom was diagnosed with Alzheimer's is guilt. I feel guilty for things I've done. I feel guilty for things I haven't done. I feel guilty for everything. I never feel like I'm doing enough to help out. I always feel like I could have done more. I feel guilty for things that I said or did to my mom before she was diagnosed with Alzheimer's. I feel guilty for things that I've said or done to my mom since she was diagnosed. I feel bad when I have to tell my dad that I can't come over to help out with my mom or that I can't call her. Even when I do go over to their house or call my mom, I never feel like it is enough.

Guilt is something that I've always struggled with throughout my life. I'm one of those people who has a hard time saying "no" to anyone. No matter how much I really don't want to do something or really don't have the time to do it, I always find myself agreeing to do things for other people. I have always felt that I would really be letting a person down if I said "no." I guess I was also a little bit afraid that the person might not like me anymore if I wasn't so willing to help out all the time. But, over the years, I have come to realize that while I am always helping everyone else out, I am constantly screwing myself. I have also realized that if a friend doesn't like me anymore simply because I am unable to do something for her, then she isn't the kind of friend I want to have anyway. I have always been there to help other people out, but I never ask for anyone's help in return. I never want to inconvenience or annoy someone by asking for help with something. I still have trouble asking for help with certain things and I still hate to inconvenience other people. Although I have gotten much better at saying "no" to people, I still feel incredibly guilty for letting them down.

This is especially true with my parents. My dad is still the full-time caregiver for my mom. I know that he is completely stressed out and overwhelmed, but, like me, he has a hard time asking for help. I often offer to help out by going over to their house to stay with my mom so that he can go to work or just to give him a break for a little while. I usually do some laundry or cleaning while I'm there and I try to do an activity with my mom, as well. There are some days or weeks that I'm unable to make it over to their house at all. My dad doesn't usually ask me to come over, but I still feel incredibly guilty for having to let him know that I won't be able to make it over for a while.

Ever since I left my job at the police department in 2013, I have felt obligated to help out. When I left my job, I never planned on not going back to work, but, here we are, three years later and I'm still not working. I know that I put most of the pressure on myself to help out and I'm sure that my dad would understand if I decided to go back to work. However, the thought of going back to a regular full-time job and never being available to help my parents out makes me feel overwhelmed with guilt. There is absolutely no way that I could do that. Plus, I would like to see where my writing takes me and that is something that I can do from home. The problem is that my house is less than ten minutes away from my parents' house, so I end up feeling obligated to go to their house to help out instead of writing at my house. I could easily tell my dad that I'm not able to come over and I often do, but I always feel guilty for doing so.

Sometimes, my dad will send me a text message and ask me to call my mom. I know that usually means that he needs a break for a few minutes. If my mom is distracted and occupied by talking to me on the phone, then my dad can get that short break. Most of the time, I have no problem giving my mom a quick call to keep her occupied for a few minutes. These conversations are not the best and we basically talk about nothing at all, but that's not the point. I know that my dad just needs me to distract her for a few minutes and I can try to have a better conversation with her another time. However, there have been times when my dad asked me to call my mom and I had to tell him "no." I've gotten these requests while I was in the middle of dinner or on my way out the door. I've also gotten these requests while I was out running errands or spending time with a friend. Even though I had a good reason for not being able to call my mom, I had pangs of guilt for having to tell my dad that I couldn't call her. It makes me feel absolutely fucking horrible to have to tell him that I can't call her. What is a measly five or ten-minute phone call out of my entire day? I'm sure that my dad is desperate for that five or ten-minute break and I can't even give it to him. I realize that I still have a life to live, but I always for so guilty for actually living it. I know that I can't be at my dad's beck and call to help out at any minute of any day, but I feel like I should be. Basically, I feel guilty any time that I'm not with my mom, talking to my mom, or helping out in some way.

Even when I am with my mom or talking to her on the phone, I still feel guilty that I'm not doing enough. I feel like my visits or phone calls aren't long enough. I feel like I get too impatient or frustrated while I am with her or talking to her. I feel like I could have done something different or something better or just something more. Nothing is ever enough. Nothing will ever be enough because nothing will cure her Alzheimer's. There is nothing I can do to fix it or make it go away, so the guilt will always be there. I can always find something to feel guilty about.

When I think back on life before my mom was diagnosed with Alzheimer's, I feel guilty for the way I sometimes treated her. I know it's ridiculous to think that any of my behaviors may have caused her illness, but I sometimes feel that way. I was a pain in the ass when I was a teenager. Most of my high school years were probably a living hell for both of my parents. I remember times when I actually screamed, "I hate you!" at my mother. I'm ashamed to admit that I ever said that to her, but I did. I remember being a disrespectful little bitch to her many times. I hated being told what to do and I made sure that she knew it. I made her life a lot more difficult than it ever had to be. I sometimes wonder if the stress that I put on her somehow increased her chances of getting Alzheimer's. Like, maybe if I had been nicer to her, then she wouldn't have gotten sick. I know that sounds ridiculous, but the thought has crossed my mind.

More so, I feel guilty for having wasted those years of her wellness being a selfish, disrespectful, pain in the ass. She was there, ready and willing to be my friend, if only I had wanted her to be. She would have done anything for me. She was (and still is) an amazing mother. And, there I was treating her like shit and taking her for granted. What a waste of absolutely precious time with her that I will never ever get back. By the time I was in my early twenties, I was less of a pain in the ass and I was ready to have a friendship with my mom. We were only a few years into our friendship phase when she was diagnosed with Alzheimer's and our whole relationship changed. If only I had known in my teen years what I know now.

What I wouldn't give for a do-over! I hate thinking about it and writing this makes me sick to my stomach. I wish I had always treated her the way I treat her now. Like gold. She never deserved to be treated like anything else. I feel incredibly guilty for having treated her so poorly and knowing that there is nothing I can do to take it back.

I also feel guilty for not being around or involved as much as I should have been when she was initially diagnosed with Alzheimer's. At 25-years-old, I was working my first real full-time job as a police officer and I was planning my wedding. I was busy, yes, but that's not an excuse. There are so many things I wish I would have asked her or talked to her about. Things that I will never have the chance to ask her now. I will never get an answer. I feel guilty that I wasn't there more to offer my help or my support. I feel guilty for never asking her how she felt, how *it* felt. I would go weeks and weeks without seeing my mom. I would go days without talking to her. I often think about what her life must have been like at the time. Having just been diagnosed with Alzheimer's disease and often home alone while my dad was at work, she must have been so scared and lonely. I have no idea how she spent her days. I should have been there. I should have at least called her. I should have never let her face those days alone. I can't even tell you how guilty I feel for not being there for her more. All I can say is that the thought of it makes me feel like absolute shit.

I could probably write an entire book about guilt. Guilt is a motherfucker. It's always there. It never goes away. I may not have these thoughts all day, every day, but, at the same time, they never leave me. They creep into my mind when I'm lying in bed at night. They sometimes keep me up for hours. They creep into my mind sometimes during a long run. They only make me run harder. They also sometimes show up unexpectedly when I simply hear the word "Alzheimer's" or read an article about it. Although I mostly try to push those pangs of guilt aside, I also think it's necessary to let them in from time to time. It makes me appreciate the relationship that I still have with my mom. It ensures that I'll never take her for granted again. It also makes me work harder to improve her quality of life now and to make myself available to help out as much as possible. Some might say that I'm being too hard on myself or that I'm beating myself up over little things. That might be true. For me, I know that these feelings of guilt are not going away anytime soon, but I'll still be sure to do as much as I can so that I have nothing to feel guilty for.

Regret

Regret, which I think ties in nicely with guilt, is another thing that I've struggled with a lot over the years. I think that most people live with some form of regret. Whether it's regretting something that we did or said, or something that we didn't do or say, regret is something that we all live with. I think the saying "live life with no regrets" is a bunch of bullshit. Try as you might, but no one is perfect and, therefore, everyone is going to regret something at some point in his/her life. It is impossible to go through your whole entire life without regretting anything. Anyone who says that they don't have any regrets is probably either high or full of shit. I mean, who the fuck do they think they're fooling anyway? Like, honestly? No one's life is all rainbows and sunshine and butterflies all the time. It's ok to have regrets. You're not always going to say or do the right thing. You're not always going to handle shit the way you should handle it. You're going to get mad at people, maybe even scream and yell at them. You're going to lose your temper and snap at people who don't deserve it. You're not going to be there for everyone when you should. You're going to lose people before you have the chance to tell them what they really mean to you. Everyone regrets things. Just be real about it.

Do I have any regrets? Hell yeah I do. I regret quitting volleyball and softball during my eighth-grade year. I regret my first choice in high schools. I regret some of the friends I've chosen and most of the guys I've dated. I regret being an intolerable, raging bitch of a teenager in high school. I regret feeling like I always had to act hard and prove that I was tough. I regret trying to be someone that I was so clearly not. I regret many of my fashion choices and some of my hairstyles. I regret screaming "I hate you" at my mom during my high school years. I even cringe now when I think about it. I regret being too cool to hang out with my family at times during high school and college. I regret spending most of my time with my friends, some of whom I would come to realize didn't deserve my time. I regret staying at a job that made me absolutely miserable for over five years. And, I also regret not going back to school or getting another job right away once I finally left that job. I regret not ending certain friendships sooner than I did. I regret wasting any amount of time thinking, worrying, and stressing about things that just simply did not matter. I sometimes, but not often, regret eating that third piece of pizza. Most of these regrets are not that big of a deal. They aren't things that I think about very often. They haven't stopped me from being happy or living my life. They are just things that most girls go through while they are growing up. Lessons learned. I was much younger and dumber back then. I know better now. However, there are certain regrets that are always on my mind. These regrets have to do with my mom's Alzheimer's.

I recently read the book "Still Alice." In the book, Alice's daughter, Lydia, asks her all sorts of questions about her Alzheimer's. Lydia asks her what it feels like to have Alzheimer's and whether or not she knows what's happening to her. She asks Alice about her symptoms and whether or not she knows when she's experiencing them. She asks Alice if she's afraid of the future and of who she will become. My mom was diagnosed with Alzheimer's almost six years ago. Granted, I don't remember every single detail from that time in our lives, but I know that I did not ask my mom any of those questions. Not a single one. How could I have not even asked her how she felt about it? What did it feel like? Was she scared? I don't remember asking her a fucking thing about it. I was too wrapped up in my own feelings about it to ask her about hers. How selfish is that? I mentioned before that my husband and I got engaged during the same month in which my mom was diagnosed. I know I was excited about getting married and planning our wedding. I know we started house hunting shortly after we got engaged. I know that I was busy working. But, what I remember most is throwing the world's biggest pity party for myself. I felt so sorry for myself that I was only 25-years-old and that my mom had just been diagnosed with Alzheimer's. I felt so sorry for myself that she wouldn't really be able to participate in much of the planning and the wedding itself. I tried to include her in things, but sometimes it was just too much. I was overwhelmed and I felt that having her there made everything that much more difficult. I was such an asshole! I never once stopped to think about how everything was affecting her and her life. It was all me, me, me, and my wedding, my wedding, my wedding. I never looked at it like it was her daughter's wedding. She wasn't able to help plan her daughter's wedding. She wasn't able to understand and participate in her own daughter's wedding. I never asked her how she felt about any of it. This was happening to *her*, not to *me*. And, I never asked her a goddamn thing. Now it's too late. I think I will regret that for the rest of my life.

During the first few years after my mom's diagnosis, I was working full time as a police officer. I honestly hated my job and my brutal hours. Even though I had three days off a week, I always spent those days catching up on things that I didn't get a chance to do while I was working. I don't think I hardly ever went to see my mom. I remember going weeks without seeing her and many days without even calling her. I'm not sure if it was just because I was so busy or if I was actively trying to avoid seeing her and having to deal with her illness. Maybe both. Either way, it kills me to think about that now. My mom was in her early 60's and she had just been diagnosed with Alzheimer's. My dad was working full time so he was gone for most of the day. Therefore, my mom sat inside her house alone, day in and day out. She was no longer allowed to drive so she couldn't go anywhere even if she wanted to. Not even to the grocery store. She just sat there alone all day, every day, while my dad was at work.

The book "Still Alice" does an excellent job of depicting the loneliness and confusion of living with Alzheimer's. It's much better than the movie, in my opinion. In the book, you're able to read Alice's thoughts throughout her lonely days at home, while her husband is at work. Mornings turn into afternoons, which turn into evenings, and then into nights. There is no concept of time or time of day. Alice starts to do something, but then she forgets what she was doing, so things are left undone all over the house. A cold cup of tea sits in the microwave. The timer continues to go off throughout the day, in an attempt to remind Alice of her tea, but Alice can't figure out where the beeping sound is coming from. She thinks it's her email, her cell phone, the house phone, or the doorbell. She thinks the black rug by the front door is a huge, gaping hole in the floor and she's afraid to go near it. She is utterly lost, scared, and confused in her own home.

It kills me to think that this might have been how my mom spent her days at home. It absolutely fucking kills me inside. I have no idea what went on during those long, lonely days. Maybe nothing at all. But maybe, she was just as lost, scared, and confused as Alice. I will never know because I wasn't there. Not only did I not bother to ask my mom about her illness and how it was affecting her, but I didn't bother to go see her. The reasons don't matter. I should have made time and I didn't. I sincerely and whole-heartedly regret not being there for my mom enough in the beginning.

My final big regret is that we didn't take a vacation with my mom after she was diagnosed with Alzheimer's. At that time, she would have been capable of enjoying a trip with her family somewhere. My mom has a long list of places that she would love to visit, but we all know that she will never get to see any of them. I wish that we would have planned a family trip somewhere shortly after she was diagnosed. But, as my husband always says, "Wish in one hand, shit in the other, and see which one fills up faster." I know that it's too late now. My mom has too much trouble getting around to be able to go on a real vacation. If we had gone shortly after she was diagnosed, she would have been able to get around just fine. She would have enjoyed it and she would have loved spending time with her family. We could have taken many pictures and made many memories. Even though she would one day forget all about it, we never would. I belong to a Facebook support group for Alzheimer's caregivers and family members. Recently, a woman posted that her husband had just been diagnosed with Alzheimer's and that she had no idea what to do now. Everyone was commenting on her post, telling her to get her affairs in order, obtain power of attorney, make a will, get him on certain medications, etc. I commented and told her to take a trip with him. I don't want her to have the same regrets that I have.

I love my mom and my life as much as the next guy, but I do have these great regrets. I don't think I will ever be able to let them go. My husband always tells me that I beat myself up and I'm too hard on myself. I guess he's right, but that's just how I feel. These are the things that go through my head. I could kick my own ass for not asking my mom about her Alzheimer's when she was actually capable of answering me. I hate myself for not being there for my mom more in the beginning of her illness. For not being more involved. For not being present. I wish we would have taken a family trip together. Wish in one hand... The regrets that I spoke of initially are things that I can easily get over. They are things that I don't think about often. The regrets that I have about my mom eat me up inside at times. I have really struggled with them over the last six years. But, I've also learned that no one is perfect and everyone is going to do or say things that they will regret. It's all part of living and learning. I just wish that I didn't have any regrets where it really counts. I will spend the rest of my mom's life and my own life trying to make it up to her.

Patience

The struggle to find my patience is an ongoing one. Having patience is probably one of the greatest struggles when learning to weather the storm of Alzheimer's. For me, having patience in general is a struggle. I am an incredibly, extremely, ridiculously impatient person. I don't like to wait more than thirty seconds for anything. I hate waiting in line for the bathroom, at the grocery store, or for the person in front of me to pick a movie from the Redbox. I cannot stand sitting in traffic or at a red light. I damn near have a major coronary event when I'm stuck behind a slow driver. I will not even briefly consider going anywhere within a ten-mile radius of the mall any time after Thanksgiving and before the end of January. Fair skin and freckles are not the only things I inherited from my Irish-as-all-hell McCafferty relatives. I am the first to admit that I have the definition of a good old Irish temper. They say, "Patience is a virtue." No truer words have ever been spoken.

Having a parent with Alzheimer's brings a whole new meaning to the phrase, "Patience is a virtue." My mom moves about as fast as a turtle crawling through peanut butter. And, I'm not just talking about physical movement. It takes her a while to mentally process things, as well. Most of the time when you ask her a question, she will just stare at you blankly. I often find myself repeating the question a few times and making sure to speak very slowly, while annunciating each word carefully. I often have to rephrase the question, testing out several different words, in order for her to understand what I'm asking her. Once she finally gets what I'm asking, it takes her just as long to form a response. She says "umm" a lot and stammers to find the right words to express her thoughts. I often joke that if I want to know what she did today or what she had for lunch, I should just ask my dad because she has to ask him first anyway. Me: "So, Mom, what did you do today?" Mom: "I don't know. Jack? JACK?! What did we do today?" Try having a full conversation like that. Ahhh!

Often worse than the mental aspect is the physical. She takes forever to walk anywhere, get dressed, use the bathroom, get in the car, etc. Normal everyday tasks take her much longer to complete. Although my mom has long forgotten how to do many things for herself, I always give her a chance to do it herself so that she can maintain some level of independence. As you may already know, a part of Alzheimer's is losing your depth perception. This particular symptom is very bad for my mom. So much so that she cannot seem to see where she is going at all. She always thinks she's walking up a hill or over a curb. She often tries to step up when she is walking on flat ground. I hold her hand or arm to guide her, but she is always hesitant and feels like she is trying to pull away from me. I'd like to strap a pair of roller skates on her feet so I could just pull her along. It can be ridiculously frustrating. I'll share an example from a few years ago.

Even though I'm not sure she fully understood what it was, my mom always wanted to go to the Philadelphia Flower Show. My dad used to take her every year, so one year I decided to take her myself to give him a break from it. I knew it would be difficult because I hate driving or parking in Philadelphia and I hate crowds, but I decided to do it anyway. We got to Philadelphia and ended up parking about three blocks away from the convention center. It probably took about twenty minutes for us to walk three blocks. My mom was walking like she was trying to tiptoe over broken glass, while barefoot, without waking anyone up. And, I was cringing the whole time as people were bumping into her and cars were flying by. We finally got to the flower show and I had to pee. So, I had to take my mom into the bathroom with me and, of course, there was a line. I'll spare you the details of our time in the bathroom, but just know that it was painfully frustrating. Once we were done with that ordeal, we walked around the flower show to look at the displays. And by walked around, I mean I held her hand so tightly that I'm sure it turned purple, as I navigated her through the crowds of people who acted like they had never seen a freaking flower before. Long story short, we bought matching t-shirts, $10 chicken Caesar salad wraps for lunch, and then painstakingly made our way back to the car to drive home. Once we were back in the car, I asked my mom if she had a good time. She said that she did, but she asked what happened to all of the flowers that were supposed to be there. Fuck me, right? At least she had a good time.

Just think, this took place a few years ago in 2012, when my mom was still in the beginning stages of Alzheimer's. Her symptoms are much more severe now than they were back then. I would not even dream of taking her to the Philadelphia Flower Show today. It is difficult enough to take her to Saladworks for lunch. In fact, taking her to Saladworks for lunch now is probably the equivalent to taking her to the Philadelphia Flower Show back then, in terms of difficulty and frustration. But, what can I say? Homegirl loves her salads.

There are times still to this day that I become so overwhelmingly frustrated and impatient with my mom that I just want to scream and yell at her. I mean, she's only in her sixties. It's not like she's in her nineties. Why is she so damn slow? Then, in a moment of calmness and clarity, I remind myself that the very things I've become so frustrated with are things that she has no control over. I tell myself, "She has fucking Alzheimer's. Why are you being such a bitch to her? Stop snapping at her! She can't help it." I try my best to be calm and patient with her, but it seems impossible at times. I'm not asking her to do much. I'm simply asking her to complete tasks that she's done on a daily basis for her whole entire life. But, that was before, and this is after. My mom is different now and she needs more time to do things. Time that I can surely afford to give her. At the end of our time out together, I tend to beat myself up for being impatient and snapping at her. I hate myself for being so rude to her and think that I ruined our time together. But, no matter how rude I've been, she always has a smile on her face and tells everyone that she had a great time with her daughter, Lauren. That always makes me feel so much better. I tell myself that there will always be a next time and I promise myself to be more patient when it comes.

Although I am definitely becoming a more patient person, I'm sure that having patience will always be a struggle for me. As my mom's condition worsens, I will need to have more and more patience. I will continue to repeat myself and to listen to her repeat herself. She will continue to do everything ever so slowly and I'll do my best not to rush her along. As time goes on, she will continue to forget how to do more things and she will need more help. Rushing her along will only upset her. And, doing everything for her will only help her forget how to do things for herself. So instead, I need to learn how to slow down and let her try to do things for herself. My mom has taught me the importance of patience and that it truly is a virtue. She has taught me that one of my biggest flaws is that I am impatient. And, at the end of the day, she makes me want to be a better person. She makes me want to be a more patient person. Not just for her, but for myself. After all, what's the rush?

Self-Pity

If you are feeling sorry for yourself for any reason right now, do yourself a favor and STOP feeling sorry for yourself. Feeling sorry for yourself will not fix the situation that is causing you to feel this way. It will not change the past or shape the future and it certainly will not make you feel any better in the long run. While you are busy throwing yourself a pity party, I can almost guarantee you that no one else even gives a shit about what you're going through. When something bad happens to us, we expect other people to feel just as badly as we do. But, we forget that people are inherently selfish. While they may feel sorry that you are going through something, I'm sure most people are just thinking to themselves how happy they are that it's not happening to them. Complain about something once or twice and you'll probably get some sympathy from people. However, when you continue to whine, cry, and complain about something all the time, you become self-indulgent, self-absorbed, and pretty fucking annoying. After all, no one likes a Negative Nancy.

Take me for example. After my mom was diagnosed with Alzheimer's in July 2010, I spent the next three years or more feeling completely sorry for myself. I had just gotten engaged in the same month that she was diagnosed, so that only added fuel to my pity fire. I cried *all* the time. I thought my world had ended. In some ways, it had. My relationship with my mom as I had always known it was over. But, I was also at a very exciting point in my life and I was about to begin a new chapter with my best friend/husband-to-be. I felt so sorry for myself that I could not even focus on the excitement of being engaged and planning a wedding. In fact, I would say that I was not at all excited about planning my wedding. All I kept thinking about was the fact that I was planning it alone. My mom was not able to help me with any of the planning. I remember crying (sad tears, not happy ones) when I went home after saying "yes" to the dress. My mom, grandmother, sister, future mother-in-law, future sister-in-law, and niece/flower girl had all come to watch me try on wedding dresses. I should have been so happy and excited. But, all I could think about was the blank expression on my mom's face as she watched me try on dresses. It was like she had no idea where we were or what we were doing or why it was such a big deal.

I picked out save-the-dates, wedding invitations, flowers, jewelry, shoes, hairstyles, you name it, all by myself. I'm pretty sure

I cried when I ordered my own "Soon-to-be Mrs. Dykovitz" zip-up hooded sweatshirt to wear on the big day. All I could think about was how my mom had gotten my sister one for Christmas the year before she got married. I was the definition of self-pity from the day I got engaged until long after my wedding day. I remember my husband asking me if I was even excited about getting married because all I did was cry that year. I felt so sorry for myself because although my mom would be there for my wedding physically, she would not be there mentally or emotionally because she could not understand or appreciate what was happening.

I was excited on my wedding day and I was able to enjoy every moment of it. I had the most perfect wedding. Everything went smoothly and it was the classy, elegant, and timeless wedding that I had hoped for. But, there were definitely moments when I would stop and watch my mom. And in those moments, I was filled with self-pity once again. She reminded me of a lost little girl, who absent-mindedly danced the night away all by herself, as if no one else was in the room. She did not seem to have a clue that she was at someone's wedding, let alone her own daughter's wedding.

After my wedding day was said and done, I continued to feel sorry for myself in many situations. "Oh, poor me, my mom can't be a part of this moment or that moment and she is incapable of being there for me the way she used to be." Gone were the days of shopping and having lunch together or going to the movies. I mean we still do those things together, but it is much different now. *I* am very much the mother and *she* is very much the daughter. I would look at other young women whose moms were always a part of everything they did and I felt completely jealous of them. I wish my mom could go to the mall and pick out a very special wedding/birthday/Christmas present for me. I wish my mom could bring soup to my house when I'm sick or surprise me by cleaning my house while I'm away on vacation. I wish my mom and I could go on a vacation together or even just a day trip. I wish my mom could have thrown me a bridal shower or a surprise 30th birthday party.

I'm not sure when it happened, but one day I woke up and realized that I had forgotten about all of those other young women. The ones whose moms died when they were young or left them when they were young. The ones whose moms were never capable of being involved in any part of their lives because of death, illness, or injury. The ones whose moms chose not to be involved in their lives. I thought about it and I realized that I was actually one of the lucky ones. I had 25 uninterrupted years with my mom, filled with love, laughter, joy, tears, shopping, lunches, movies, surprises, and memories. I still have my mom, even though our relationship is much different now. And, she did not choose for it to be this way. She did not leave me or choose to ignore me. She has never done anything, but love me. Therefore, I am one of the lucky ones and definitely not someone who should be wallowing in self-pity all day, every day.

I realized that I had become an annoying, whiny, sad, and weak woman. I was incapable of ever being happy about anything because I could not stop thinking about what I had lost. How could my husband even stand to be with me anymore? I was a far cry from the strong, sassy, hard-ass, smart-mouthed 23-year-old girl who he had met and fallen in love with. The girl who would always try her best and never give up. The girl who ran her heart out and left most of the guys trailing behind her. I realized that I had to get that girl back. It was then that I signed up for a half-marathon to raise money for the Alzheimer's Association. I went from telling maybe one person outside of my family about my mom's Alzheimer's to telling the whole world. I posted about it on Facebook and began to talk openly about it to anyone who would listen. I saw the generosity of people who barely knew me, but still donated to my cause. I realized that I had wasted a lot of time feeling sorry for myself when what I should have been doing was sharing my story with others. I should have been raising awareness and taking action against Alzheimer's. The younger version of me would have never sat back and allowed herself to get beat down by anyone or anything. She would have fought back. So, that's what I decided to do. Rather than sit back and let Alzheimer's beat me down, I was going to fight back. I was going to raise awareness by sharing my story with others. I was going to take action by raising money and participating in events that raise money for Alzheimer's. And, I was never going to sit around feeling sorry for myself again. If Alzheimer's was going to try to take me down, I would be going down swinging.

Self-pity has its place and its appropriate time. You're allowed to feel sorry for yourself when life knocks you down. But, only for a very short time. If you continue to feel sorry for yourself for a long period of time, you are doing yourself a disservice. As far as I know, self-pity has never solved anyone's problems. No one wants to listen to you whine and complain about your problems unless you're going to do something about it. So, instead of wasting your time feeling sorry for yourself, why don't you put your time and energy into doing something about it? There will always be someone who is far worse off than you. The sooner you realize this, the better, because self-pity looks good on no one.

Finding My Strength

I wrote this particular section while sitting in the Atlanta airport with at least an hour to kill before my flight back to Alabama. As I sat there ignoring the hustle and bustle of everyone around me, I was deep in thought. My recent trip home to Delaware to visit my parents had really got me thinking about how much our lives had changed since my mom was diagnosed with Alzheimer's over five years ago. Five years? Is that all it had been? It seemed like a lifetime ago. So much had changed in five years. My mom is a dramatically different person now than she was back then. So is my dad. I can't even begin to imagine what our lives will be like in another five years. Or five months for that matter.

Five years ago, my mom was walking and talking and eating and doing things for herself almost like a normal person. There were slight differences, but they were only visible to her closest family members. Five years ago, I couldn't imagine myself doing half of the shit that I do for her now. I couldn't imagine having to help her walk or get into the car. I couldn't imagine having to show her where the bathroom is in her own house and then helping her use it, telling her to make sure that she pulls her underwear down so she doesn't pee through them. I couldn't imagine having to cut her food up into tiny little pieces and show her how to eat it. I couldn't imagine having to help her get dressed like a four-year-old. I couldn't imagine having to talk... like... this... just... so... she... could... understand... me. If you had asked me five years ago, I would have told you that I wouldn't be capable of doing any of the things that I do for her now. The same goes for now when I try to envision what our lives will be like in five years. I can't imagine myself being capable of doing the things that I'm sure I will have to do for my mom in another five years.

I am incredibly lucky to have very sweet, supportive friends at home in Delaware. During one of my trips home from Alabama, I was able to spend time with some of them. During a conversation over cheese, pretzel bites, and pizza (don't judge!), we were talking about my mom and how she was doing. I mentioned that I thought she might be on the verge of incontinence because she never knew when she had to use the bathroom. I would ask her if she had to go and she would say that she didn't. I would ask her to try to go anyway and she would agree. Then, I'd stand outside the bathroom door and listen to her peeing. So, she did have to go to the bathroom, but she didn't recognize the feeling that she had to go. I'm not an expert, but I believed that this meant that she would probably become incontinent in the near future. I was telling my friends that I could never imagine myself changing my mom's diapers someday and how difficult that would be. I told them that I didn't want to have to do that for my mom and that I hoped I wouldn't have to. Then, my dear friend, with tears in her eyes, said, "I know that you don't want to do it, but I think that you will be able to. When that day comes, you will just do it." With tears in my own eyes, I said, "I don't want to have to do that for my mom. I wish I wouldn't have to do that someday. I don't want that to be my life."

After we wiped our tears, watched Magic Mike 2 in our Snuggies, and ate donuts (again, don't judge!), I got to thinking. My sweet friend was right. I think back to all of the things I once said I didn't want to have to do for my mom five years ago. I do all of those things now. I still don't want to have to change my mom's diapers or feed her pureed food one day, but I know I will do it. Somehow, I will find the strength to do it for my mom. I'm sure that it will be very difficult at first. I have a feeling that I will go through the entire grieving process again. When your loved one has Alzheimer's, you are constantly grieving new losses. You lose a little bit more of them each day. Then, you eventually become accustomed to the new loss and begin to accept it. But, it won't be long before you lose a little bit more and you begin the grieving process all over again. Caring for someone with Alzheimer's means that your life is changing constantly. You learn to adapt to these changes just in time for new changes to arrive. Change and adapt. Change and adapt. Change and adapt. That's just the way it goes.

I think that it is amazing what we can adapt to throughout our lives. We can become used to doing things that we could have never imagined ourselves doing before we were suddenly doing them. After a while, it becomes no big deal. We adapt ourselves and our lives to the changes around us. The thing is that we are always capable of doing more than we think we can do. It really is true that you don't know how strong you are until being strong is the only choice you have. It never gets any easier, but you always get stronger. Five years ago, I never thought that I was strong enough to handle the things that I do for my mom now. Back then, I couldn't even look at my mom without tearing up and having to leave the room to cry. Now, I smile when I look at her. She's still the same person, but she just needs help with a lot of things. I know that she feels safe with me and that she appreciates my help.

I'm sure that there will come a time in the future when I no longer smile when I look at her. I'm sure that I will tear up and have to leave the room to cry again. But, I also know that I will smile again. The changes will come and it will suck and I will cry a lot. But then, I will adapt and grow stronger and smile again, eventually. I'm still afraid of what the future holds for us, but I know that I'll be able to handle it. It will be difficult at first, but I will adapt and overcome the challenges I am faced with. You never know how much you're capable of doing until you try. What I do know is that love wins every time. The love I have for my mom will help me to find the strength I need to handle whatever presents itself. For my mom, I will adapt and overcome. For my mom, I will find my strength. I will be STRONG.

The Longest Goodbye

When I was living in Alabama, about 900 miles away from home, my mom and I relied heavily on phone conversations to keep in touch. I tried to call my mom every two or three days and talk for at least thirty minutes. As her Alzheimer's progressed, it became increasingly more difficult to have a conversation with my mom. I have always found that it was much easier to talk to her in person because we could see each other, which seemed to cause less confusion for her. Talking on the phone was a whole different story. She didn't seem to understand that even though she was talking to me, I was still in Alabama. When we talked on the phone, she always thought that I was actually there with her in Delaware. It was often a struggle to keep her talking on the phone for more than ten minutes. She never knew what to talk about and had a difficult time trying to follow along with what I was talking about. Therefore, I was very limited with what I could tell her or ask her about. Many times, it was like pulling teeth to have an actual conversation with her. But, I knew that if I talked about Oakley and Lucy, she would follow along easily and enjoy every minute of our conversation. It was a good thing that they provided constant entertainment and a never-ending supply of stories for me to tell her.

The end of our phone conversations was always the same. I told her that it was time for me to hang up and she would say, "Ok." That was followed by the longest goodbye in the history of phone conversations of anyone ever. It usually went something like this:

Me: "Ok, Mom, I have to get going now."

Mom: "Ok."

Me: "Alright, so I love you, have a good day, and I'll talk to you soon."

Mom: "Ok. Alright. I love you, too."

Me: "Ok, bye, Mom."

Mom: "Ok, bye. I love you. Tell Steve and the babies I love them. Lucy and…. what's the other one's name again?"

Me: "Oakley and Lucy."

Mom: "Oakley! That's right. And Lucy. Like the TV show, 'I Love Lucy.' You know that's back on TV now?"

Me: "Oh really? No, I didn't know that. Ok, Mom. I love you."

Mom: "I love you, too. Have a good day…night…what time of day is it?"

Me: "It's the afternoon, Mom, so you can say, 'Have a good day.'"

Mom: "Ok, have a good day. I love you. Tell everyone I love them and I said, 'Hi.'"

Me: "Ok, Mom. I will let them all know. I love you, too. I'll talk to you soon."

Mom: "Ok…talk to you soon…When are you coming home again?"

Me: "I'll be home to visit soon and I'll be home for good in January."

Mom: "Oh, January?! That's great. My birthday is January 24th."

Me: "Yes, Mom. I know it is. Ok, I have to go. I'll call you soon."

Mom: "Ok. I love you. Bye."

Me: "Love you, too, Mom. Bye."

Mom: "Ok. Drive carefully."

Me: "Ok. I will."

Mom: "See ya later, alligator."

Me: "Ok. Talk to you soon. Love you. Bye."

Mom: "I love you, too, sweetheart. Bye."

Me: "BYE!"

And then, we finally hung up. This is not an exaggeration. Sometimes our goodbyes lasted even longer than that. When I hung up the phone, I always closed my eyes, took a deep breath, and let that shit go. FUCK!!! That was the longest goodbye ever! I knew it wasn't her fault, but god damn! It took longer to say goodbye to her than it did to have an entire conversation with her. I knew part of it was that she had forgotten how to have a conversation or how to properly say goodbye. I also thought that she was afraid that she was forgetting to tell me something, so she would stall. She tried to keep me on the phone so she could remember what she was supposed to say. I tried my best to be patient with her, but it was very difficult sometimes. I knew it wasn't her fault. Sometimes, I would start laughing and joking with her about how long it took her to say goodbye. Now, I have learned to appreciate the fact that she is still able to speak and have a conversation with me, even if it isn't always a great one. I know the day will come when she's no longer able to have verbal communication and I will wish that we were on the phone having one of our longest goodbyes ever.

Actually, Alzheimer's is really the longest goodbye. Even longer than our goodbyes at the end of our phone conversations. I've been saying goodbye to my mom since at least July 2010, which is when she was diagnosed with Alzheimer's. I've probably been saying goodbye to her since even before then, but I just didn't know it yet. I say goodbye to pieces of my mom every single day. Each day, I lose more and more of her, as she loses more and more of herself. Often times, she is just an empty shell of the person she used to be. She has lost the ability to remember facts, names, events, and information. She has lost the ability to find her way around her house, use the bathroom without assistance, and dress herself. She needs help showering and grooming herself. She needs someone to get her food and something to drink. She needs someone to cut up her food so she can eat it. She needs to drink from a cup with a lid and a straw. She is losing her ability to walk, especially more than ten feet, but she refuses the assistance of a wheelchair or walker. She has pretty much lost her ability to think, reason, and solve problems, although she has some moments of clarity. She is losing her ability to have a conversation more and more each day. She is losing every piece of herself, slowly and painfully, until there is nothing left.

I hate it when people have the balls to say to me, "Well, at least you know she's not suffering. She's not in pain." My mom may not be in physical pain, but she is definitely suffering. She is dying from an illness for which there is no cure. Alzheimer's is terminal. There is NO cure. There are NO survivors. She has been dying for over five years now. And, yes, I do believe that my mom is aware of what is happening to her. Maybe she's not aware of it all the time, but, at times, she is definitely aware. She tells people that she has a memory problem and she gets frustrated with herself when she can't remember something. She is aware. Do you have any idea how much it sucks to see her struggle like that? Honestly, I don't think anyone knows what it's like unless they've been there.

There are times when I think to myself, "I wish she had cancer instead. I know that she's going to die from Alzheimer's and I just want to get it over with." I realize that this probably sounds harsh to some people, but I'm not here to sugarcoat anything. This is how I actually feel. I've been watching my mom die at an excruciatingly slow pace for the last five years. Since she is only 68-years-old, she could live for another five to ten years before she dies from this disease. And, she WILL die from this disease. She is young enough that her body is completely healthy. There is nothing wrong with her. She will die after Alzheimer's has stripped her of every ounce and fiber of her being. She will die when Alzheimer's has had enough of her and leaves her for dead. She will die a very long, slow, painful, and tragic death. How could I not wish that she had cancer or another disease that might kill her more quickly? I would much rather her have a short, sweet goodbye than a long, brutal one.

I don't think there is anything in this world to prepare you for the death of a loved one. Whether it is expected or unexpected. Sudden or a long time coming. I think that if I know we're going to be saying goodbye, I'd rather just get it over with. I hate saying goodbye. I hate the build-up to it and I hate the production of actually saying goodbye. Well, I've been saying goodbye to my mom for over five years now. And, she still doesn't have her coat on, her purse in her hand, or even one foot out the door. This is truly the longest goodbye. Alzheimer's is truly the longest goodbye. In many ways, I've already said goodbye to my mom. I've said goodbye to many pieces of the mother who raised me. She is almost completely gone now. Gone, but still here. How do you grieve the loss of someone who is still standing right in front of you? There is no closure. There is no moving on. The mother who stands before me now is much more like a child than a mother. I must continue to care for and say goodbye to the physical being of my mom. Many parts of her are gone and I've somewhat made my peace with that, but yet she still remains.

I've read that you grieve two losses when you lose someone to Alzheimer's. You grieve the loss of the person you once knew and then you grieve the loss of their actual, physical body. Well, that's pretty fucked up. Two losses equal two goodbyes. Two very long goodbyes. The longest goodbyes ever. I've already said goodbye to the mom I once knew, but I still continue to say goodbye to the mom standing before me. Neither of these goodbyes have been easy and I feel like I will never be done saying goodbye to either one of my moms. I guess it is something that will come with time. If nothing good comes from saying the longest goodbye, at least I have learned a lot from it. I've learned to appreciate saying the longest goodbye at the end of our phone conversations because one day the longest goodbye will be the last goodbye.

Still Jerie

As I previously discussed, one of the things I've struggled with the most is loving the stranger that my mom has become. I firmly believe that struggles and challenges make us stronger and teach us valuable life lessons. My struggle with learning to love my new mom has taught me that my old mom is still in there somewhere. This stranger who has seemingly replaced my mom is still my mom. She is still Jerie.

Many times, people with Alzheimer's disease are forgotten. Sometimes, it occurs long before the official diagnosis has been received. Friends or family members start noticing changes in their loved one and they may not know how to address these changes. Often times, it is easier to forget about the person and simply move on without trying to figure out what is really going on. Other times, once the official diagnosis is obtained, it is just too much to bare.

Friends or family members, even neighbors, are not sure how to react to the diagnosis or how to interact with the Alzheimer's patient. They often become scared of that person. They are scared of the unknown. Again, it is easier to forget about the person and move on. An Alzheimer's diagnosis is only the beginning of a very long, rocky road, filled with ups and downs, peaks and valleys, and unfamiliar terrain. It is difficult to travel along this road and to witness firsthand how the journey destroys the person you love. Rather than deal with it all, many people find it easier to just walk away. But, my mom is still Jerie, the woman we all know and love, and she should not be forgotten, discarded, or written off just because of some stupid fucking disease.

Unfortunately, I have experienced this firsthand through my mom's struggle with Alzheimer's. Not with close family members, as my family has been very supportive and helpful, but I have noticed it with more distant family members. Family members who may not have seen my mom in years, but are aware that she has Alzheimer's, do not know how to approach her. Many times, they expect my mom to still know who they are and to know how they are related to the family. I'm sorry, but my mom has no fucking clue who you are. She even sometimes forgets people that she sees frequently, so how is she supposed to remember the distant family members that she hasn't seen in years?

Once people introduce themselves to my mom and she clearly does not remember them, they begin shouting their names at her as if that's going to jog her memory. She has Alzheimer's. She's not deaf. Shouting at her is not going to do anything except make her feel stupid and anxious because she does not remember you. I often tell people to tell my mom their full name and explain how they are related to the family. You should just assume that she does not remember you and explain who you are right off the bat. This makes for an easier and less stressful introduction, as well as an easy transition into a conversation with her. That's right, a conversation. Don't just simply introduce yourself and then turn your back on her. Or, worse, talk about her as if she isn't there. Would you do that to someone who has cancer? No, because that would make you an asshole. Same goes with Alzheimer's. Ignoring her or talking about her like she isn't there still makes you an asshole.

Many people just assume that my mom has nothing to contribute to a conversation so they just ignore her. Sure, that's much easier than struggling through a conversation with her, but I can't tell you how happy it would make my mom for you to just talk to her. I know for a fact that she often feels ignored and excluded during social gatherings. And, I have to admit that she often *is* ignored and excluded. No one knows how to approach her or what to say to her. They are often clearly uncomfortable with the situation and would rather stay away. But remember, she's still Jerie. She can still talk your ear off about god knows what and she's guaranteed to make you smile if you give her a chance. Luckily, this problem only occurs once in a while, usually at events like weddings and funerals, which are both pretty much out of the question for my mom at this point anyway. It's just too much unnecessary stress on her. Most people could spare a few minutes of their time to talk to my mom, especially since they won't see her again until the next family gathering. A few minutes of their time would mean more to my mom than they could ever know.

My mom's friends and neighbors have much more obviously forgotten about her. I'm not sure when exactly it occurred, before or after her diagnosis, but they dropped her like a hot potato. People stopped calling and stopping by. The only people who go to my parents' house, other than for a family gathering, are me, my husband, my sister, my brother-in-law, my Aunt Diane (my mom's sister), and my Aunt Elaine (my dad's sister). No one else visits them or stops by the house to offer their help in any way. Literally no one. Not one friend or neighbor. Not even so much as a casserole dish left on the front doorstep. They also stopped inviting my mom out to lunch or to go shopping. Eventually, her friends became non-existent.

Maybe it's because she was no longer allowed or able to drive once she was diagnosed with Alzheimer's. Maybe it's because they noticed changes in her behavior that made them uncomfortable. Or, maybe they just simply did not know how to deal with her disease and its inevitable devastation. Alzheimer's is a very difficult disease to deal with, understandably so. But, would you drop someone as a friend if you found out he/she had cancer? Again, no, because that would make you an asshole. I'm sure you would offer to help the cancer patient and his/her family in any way that you could. I know that's exactly what people did when my mom had breast cancer. (Yup, that's right, she had cancer, too. Double whammy.) But, the way people treated her then and the way people treat her now is vastly different. And, I know why.

I hate to phrase it this way, but cancer is a "sexy" disease. The media has made it "sexy" and it has become trendy to raise awareness and take action for cancer. Alzheimer's is not a "sexy" disease. It's a mental disease. It scares people. There is absolutely no way to make it a "sexy" disease. Most people think that only old people get Alzheimer's and old people are generally not considered to be "sexy." There's nothing "sexy" about a person with Alzheimer's. There's nothing "sexy" about someone who doesn't shower, wash their hair, or brush their teeth. There's nothing "sexy" about someone who dresses in mismatched clothing, with food stains down the front of it, which is most likely on inside-out or backwards. There's nothing "sexy" about an adult who wears diapers and has to have their food cut up into small pieces or pureed so that they can eat it without choking to death. Cancer is the popular kid in high school who eats lunch with the "in" crowd, while Alzheimer's is the geeky kid with acne and braces who eats alone, and no one even notices her.

Since Alzheimer's is not trendy or "sexy", most people don't know anything about it, which is probably why my mom's friends and neighbors have forgotten all about her. No one offers to help in any way at all. No one cooks meals and drops them off to my parents' house like they did when she had cancer. No one calls her or my dad to see how they're doing. No one stops by to visit my mom, even though some of her neighbors are home all day. No one offers to sit with my mom for a little while so that my dad can run an errand. No one bothers to wave to the crazy old lady who is staring aimlessly out the front door. I know that my mom would love nothing more than for an old friend or neighbor to stop by to see her. Admittedly, it would probably confuse the hell out of her, but she would still love it. She would love for someone to make her feel wanted or for someone to make it a point to catch up with her. Who cares if she doesn't make any sense when she's talking to you? Or, if she can't tell you what she's been up to or what she did last weekend? Just let her babble on and on anyway. It would make her so happy just to feel acknowledged. To make her feel like she is still Jerie.

I believe that if people knew more about Alzheimer's, then they would be more likely to keep in touch with a family member, friend, or neighbor who has the disease. They wouldn't be so scared or turned off by it. They would want to help out as much as they want to help their friend who's been battling cancer for years. They would understand that an Alzheimer's patient is still a person. A person with feelings, interests, opinions, beliefs, and stories to tell. My mom may have Alzheimer's disease. She may continue to decline at a painfully slow rate over the next ten years or more. She may eventually forget about all of the people who have already forgotten about her and the ones who never will. She may not ever be the fully functioning woman that she once was, but she is still Jerie.

It took me a while to learn this myself. It took me a while to look past the Alzheimer's and see the person hiding deep inside. But, now I know that the person inside is still my mom. She is still Jerie. She is still a wife, mother, daughter, sister, aunt, and friend. She still cares more about everyone else than she does about herself. She still only sees the good in others and has a kind, generous heart. She is still an animal lover. She still loves music and dancing and being around people she loves. She still loves her man Elvis. She still likes to talk about American history, even if she gets most of the facts wrong. She still loves to get her hair and nails done with her daughters. She would still rather spend time with her husband than anyone else. She is still a better person than most people could ever hope to be. She deserves to be acknowledged and included. She deserves to be respected and spoken to. She deserves to feel useful and to have a purpose. She deserves to be given a chance. And, she deserves to be remembered and loved. Because, at the end of the day, Alzheimer's and all, she is still Jerie.

Lowering My Expectations

Over the years, I have learned that lowering my expectations of my mom as her Alzheimer's progresses is extremely beneficial for both of us. I cannot expect the same things out of my mom now as I once did. It can be a heartbreaking thought, but it is reality. I still often wonder what our adult relationship as mother and daughter would be like if she didn't have Alzheimer's. I think about what it would be like to get a text or an email from her. What would it be like to receive a card for St. Patrick's Day from her? Or any other random holiday for that matter? What would it be like to receive a card from her that I knew she had carefully chosen herself instead of knowing that my dad had picked it out? What would it be like to be able to actually read what she wrote inside of that card? I often think about how different it would be to go to lunch, shopping, or to the movies with her now if she didn't have Alzheimer's. Maybe she would pick me up from my house and we would chit chat the whole way to the restaurant and throughout our meal. Maybe I wouldn't have to stare at her, racking my brain to find something, anything, to talk to her about. Our phone conversations wouldn't be one-sided like they are now. I wouldn't have to buy and wrap Christmas presents for my dad from her and sneak them under their tree. I wouldn't have to go into a bathroom stall with her to show her what to do and help her do it. I wouldn't have to cut her food up for her to eat or hold her hand while we're walking somewhere. I could go on and on.

These constant thoughts of what once was and what might have been are enough to drive me insane. If that's all I ever think about, I'm sure to ruin our time together. Every phone call, conversation, or day out will always come up short. The holidays and birthdays will never be good enough. I will always leave her feeling empty and unfulfilled. I'm setting our "new" relationship up for failure. But, what if it didn't have to be that way? What if I gave my mom a little credit and cut her a lot of slack? By lowering my expectations of her and our time together, there is hope that it will be better than I had anticipated. It might seem harsh to say, but now, I don't expect anything at all from her. When she forgets my birthday, I can't be upset with her because I don't expect her to remember it anyway. I can't even tell you how much it meant to me that on my 30th birthday, not only did she call me, but she sang "Happy Birthday" to me. And, she remembered all the words. Although that made my birthday special, I would never expect it to happen again and, so far, it hasn't.

In the past, I would often call my mom and expect to have this great, long conversation with her. But now, I don't expect anything at all from our conversations other than that she will probably ask me the same thing thirty-seven times. I would say that nine times out of ten, our conversations are basically meaningless and unfulfilling. But, that tenth conversation, the one where we really connect and she seems totally with it, just means *that* much more to me. My mom and I will often go to get our hair done together. I'll pick her up and we'll drive to our long-time stylist/family friend's house. I used to always have these high expectations. I would stop to get us hot chocolate before I picked her up, but she wouldn't touch it and it would just get cold. I would expect great conversations and a great lunch together. One time at lunch, I got so upset over something so stupid that I got her up and we walked out of the restaurant without even eating. I beat myself up over it for a long time and told myself that I would never do that again. My expectations of our lunches out are much lower now. And, guess what. I have never made her leave a restaurant again. We always have a nice lunch and she always raves about how good her salad was, even though she has the exact same thing every time we go.

My point is that I cannot expect the same behavior out of my mom now that she has Alzheimer's. There are many things that she is no longer able to do. I would be an ignorant asshole if I thought any differently. My mom needs help with most of her daily activities. She needs help showering, dressing, using the bathroom, eating, walking, getting into a car, finding her way around her house, etc. As her Alzheimer's progresses, my expectations of her change accordingly. At this point, I don't expect anything from her at all. I don't expect her to be able to do anything for herself without needing a lot of assistance. I just always assume that she will need me to do every single thing for her, but I always still give her the opportunity to try for herself. She needs to continue to try doing things for herself so that she can maintain some level of independence, confidence, and purpose. And, if she is unable to do a certain task herself, then I am right there, ready and willing to do it for her. No judgement. No expectations. No disappointments.

Having high expectations of my mom will only make her feel inadequate and myself unfulfilled. By lowering my expectations, I find that I am often pleasantly surprised. My best friend once told me that everything doesn't always have to be so perfect. She is so right. Many great things in life come from imperfection. My mom is going to have more bad days than good in terms of her illness. Why make those bad days any worse by putting unfair pressure on her or our time together to be perfect? No matter what, I guarantee you that my mom thinks our time together *is* perfect. She never has a bad time when she spends it with those she loves. By lowering my expectations, I am allowing her to be exactly who she is now and I'm not putting any pressure on her to be different. I'm not disappointed when something doesn't go right or I don't get anything out of it. The good days and the moments of clarity are that much better when they come unexpectedly. The lower my expectations are, the greater the chance is that she will surprise me. And, let me tell you, she is full of surprises.

As Long as She's Happy

One thing I've learned about Alzheimer's and caregiving is that no two experiences are the same. Alzheimer's patients are like snowflakes. Every single one is different. When it comes to caring for a loved one with Alzheimer's, you have to find what works best for you. Sure, there are plenty of proven methods and tips for caregiving, but you have to tailor your caregiving to fit your needs. You know your loved one best and you will be able to determine the best way to care for him/her. It might involve a bit of trial and error, but that's ok. Alzheimer's caregiving is a learning process.

I have read many articles and Facebook posts about the benefits that certain things may have on an Alzheimer's patient. I've read about the importance of an Alzheimer's patient having a set routine and a healthy diet, as well as getting some level of physical and mental exercise. I've read about the importance of maintaining personal hygiene, such as showering and washing her hair regularly. I've also read about how eliminating sugar and white bread from her diet and slathering her entire body in coconut oil every day will improve her symptoms. Well, I call bullshit on that one. But, I do know that *some* of these things are important and *some* have been proven to be beneficial to *some* people. Some, some, some. Not all.

I'm not an expert on Alzheimer's, but I am an expert on my mom. I know what she likes and doesn't like. I know what will work with her and what will not. Although I am not a full-time caregiver, I take my part-time caregiving responsibilities very seriously. I have tried different approaches and activities with my mom over the years. Some things have worked. Other things were utter failures. Many times, I feel like I have absolutely no idea what the fuck I'm doing. But, the best part is that my mom has no idea what I'm doing either. All she knows is that I'm spending time with her and that makes her happy. I have learned over the years that no matter what I do, all that really matters is that she's happy. As long as she's happy, I must be doing something right. As long as she's happy, then whatever I'm doing for her is enough. I'm sure that some people would disagree with that. I'm sure that some nursing homes and professional caregivers would insist on doing more things for my mom, some of which might make her unhappy. They might insist on washing her hair at least once a week and not allowing her to eat sweets. Maybe those things are important and maybe they would help. But, this isn't a nursing home and I'm not a professional caregiver. This is life and I do what I can.

In my mind, as long as she's happy, then I'm doing enough. As long as she's happy, who cares if her hair is dirty, greasy, and unwashed? As long as she's happy, who cares if her breath smells bad? As long as she's happy, who cares if she drinks soda instead of water and eats cookies instead of fruit? Honestly, I could give a shit what she's eating or drinking as long as she's eating and drinking period. I will usually try to push the water on her over a Diet Coke, but if she refuses something a third time, then I back off. I will offer her a healthy snack over junk food, but if she insists on eating cookies instead, then homegirl wants some damn cookies! I have definitely learned my limits with her.

Unfortunately, I learned my limits the hard way. One time during a visit home from Alabama, I gave my dad a break by helping my mom get ready for bed at night. She had already used the bathroom and put her pajamas on, so I told her to brush her teeth. She looked at me like I was crazy and said that she had already brushed them that day. Apparently, she only brushed her teeth in the morning and that was it for the day. I thought that was disgusting and I was a little annoyed at my dad for not insisting that she brush her teeth again at night. I told my mom that she should really brush her teeth at least twice a day and that she needed to brush them before bed. She refused again and I kept insisting that she brush them. We ended up arguing about it a little bit and I could tell that she was getting really mad at me. I finally gave up and helped her get into bed without brushing her teeth.

The next morning, my dad told me that my mom woke up feeling upset and that she kept asking him if he was mad at her. She kept saying that she thought they had an argument the night before and that he was upset with her. My dad said that my mom was really upset and confused about it. I realized that she must have been talking about when we argued about her brushing her teeth the night before. I felt terrible for causing her to be so upset and confused. I felt even worse that she was blaming my dad for it. I have never and will never again insist on her doing something if she adamantly refuses to do it.

I have definitely learned to choose my battles carefully. Most of the time, it's just not worth the fight. Whenever my husband is annoying the shit out of me, I glare at him and say, "Don't poke the bear." I've found that it's quite effective. I guess I have developed this same mentality with my mom. I have learned that when she says "no" she means "no." It is almost never worth the argument to try to convince her otherwise. I have learned not to poke the bear. I have learned to let sleeping dogs lie. As long as she's happy, then I'm happy. Alzheimer's has already taken so much from my mom. It has stripped her of her memories and her independence. It has taken away the ability for her to think and do for herself. The last thing I want is for it to take away her happiness, as well. I'm not an expert on this disease. I don't have all of the answers. I'm not the perfect caregiver. But, my mom is happy. And, as long as she's happy, I don't give a damn about anything else.

The Balancing Act

When I started helping take care of my mom a few years ago, I learned how I should act around her. I've learned to speak slowly, clearly, and positively. I've learned not to argue with her about anything. I've learned not to question or correct her when she tells me stories that don't quite sound right. I've learned not to ask her if she remembers things, but rather to remind her of them. I've learned to hold her hand and guide her to places instead of simply giving her commands and telling her where to go. I've learned a lot about being a caregiver, but I am still learning.

One thing I'm still learning is how to balance being a caregiver and just being myself. It is often difficult to know where my role of being a caregiver ends and my role of being myself begins. Being a caregiver does not define who I am, but it is a large part of me. Remember, I was just 25-years-old when my mom was diagnosed with Alzheimer's. I was only 28-years-old when I quit my job as a police officer and started caring for my mom part-time. Through much of my twenties, I had no idea who I was or who I wanted to be. Like most 20-somethings, I was still trying to figure that all out. I was trying to find myself. My journey of self-discovery helped me realize and accept that I no longer wanted to be a police officer. It also helped me realize that I wanted to spend more time with my mom and be able to help take care of her. Becoming a caregiver for my mom further shaped the woman I am today. But, I am not just a caregiver. That role does not define me as a person. I am still Lauren. I still need to be myself. But, there are many times when I'm not sure which role I should be playing.

Whenever there is a family party, my husband and I will usually pick my parents up and give them a ride. Since we all arrive at the party together, I usually take over the caregiver role for the remainder of the party. I know that my dad wants to have a few Coors Lights and relax for a change. I also know that he needs and deserves that "time off" much more than I do. Therefore, I don't mind taking over the caregiver role for the night and allowing my dad to have a good time. However, it's a little difficult to play both the caregiver and myself for the night. I want to be caring, patient, and attentive for my mom, but I also want to be loud, funny, and potty-mouthed for my other family members. I want to be the caregiver, while also just being myself. It may not seem like it, but it's very hard to find the balance between the two roles. How can I tell my family members funny stories without making my mom feel left out because she doesn't understand what I'm talking about? How can I hang out with everyone in the kitchen without leaving my mom sitting all by herself in the living room? How can I make sure that my mom is included and involved in what's going on even though she has no clue what's going on? How can I get my mom something to eat or drink and help her use the bathroom without completely missing out on all of the family fun? Some people might say that it is not solely my responsibility to take care of my mom at family parties and that I should try to enjoy myself. But, I would rather sit in a room alone with my mom while everyone else has fun than leave my mom sitting alone, staring off into space, just so I can have a good time.

That's when the balancing act comes into play. How can I be both the patient, attentive caregiver and still have fun being myself? It's a balance and it's not easy. Often times, family parties are quite stressful for me because they involve an awful lot of work for me. I can't just simply float around the party, smiling and chatting with everyone. I am usually right by my mom's side the entire time in order to help her with things and to make her feel included in the party. I feel obligated to do this. There is no shutting it off for me. There is no clocking out. It is just what I must do in order to protect her and take care of her. I do my best to balance both roles. I stay close to my mom's side to help her and let her know that she's not being ignored. But, I also try to talk to everyone at the party and have a good time. Like I said, it's a lot of work and it can be very stressful. There are many times when I would much rather just skip the party completely. Of course, I want to see my family and spend time with them, but it would be much easier to just avoid the whole situation. This is especially true for bigger events, such as weddings, bridal showers, or baby showers. However, I know that there will come a day when my mom's attendance at such events will be completely out of the question, so, for now, I will continue to do my best balancing act.

Aside from balancing the roles of being a caregiver and being myself, it is difficult to balance my parents' needs and my own needs. My mom needs a lot of help and is unable to take care of herself anymore. My dad needs a lot of help with taking care of my mom. I am usually the only person willing, able, and available to help them out. As I said before, I also feel obligated to help them. I feel as though it is my duty as their daughter to help them. I am a doer, a fixer, a helper. I would feel like total shit if I did nothing to help out my own mom and dad. Worse than the stress of helping them out is the guilt that I would feel if I did nothing to help. I don't understand how someone in my position could not feel obligated to help out. I don't feel as though I'm doing anything noble or admirable. I am simply doing what I should do.

Having said all of that, it is difficult to draw the line between helping my parents and helping myself. My husband often reminds me that I am still young and that I have my own life to live. He tells me that I deserve to have a life and a career of my own choosing. He tells me that I deserve to have fun with my friends and to take some time off from taking care of my mom. I know that he's right, but it's hard for me to put myself before my parents. I don't think that I could ever go back to working a regular full-time job because I know that I wouldn't have any time to help out with my mom. Maybe I am being unfair to myself, but I know that I would never forgive myself if I wasn't around to help out. I know that I deserve to have a successful, fulfilling career, but I would never choose that career over my mom. I think it is a lot like when a new mom decides to stay at home with her kids rather than go back to work. I have the rest of my life to work and make money, but I might only have a few more years left to spend time with my mom. I want to make sure that I make those years count. I want to make the last few years of her life the best that they can possibly be. I often think that if all I do is help take care of my mom, then I will have nothing to show for my life once she's gone. But, at the same time, I will have learned a lot from my time with her and I will be able to share that with others. I will have so much to offer other people who are going through what I have already gone through. So, in that sense, helping my parents through this storm will also help me fulfill my purpose in the long run.

Life is often a balancing act for many of us. We have to prioritize and figure out what works best for ourselves. We have to find our own balance. I'm still learning to find my balance. I'm still learning to live my own life in the midst of this horrific storm. But, I know that I will have plenty of time to live my life to its fullest once we come out of this storm. For now, I don't think I'm meant to be living my life for just me. I'm meant to be living it for all of us. The thought of that brings me peace. And, it is in that peace that I know I have found my balance.

Remembering

Alzheimer's is a bitch. If it were a person, she would be the mean girl in high school who fucked with you just because she could. Just when you think that she might start to leave you alone, she steals your best friend. Alzheimer's has done just that. She has stolen one of my best friends. She has fucked with me so much over the last almost six years. Just when I think that she might leave me alone for a while, that she might take it easy on me, here she comes strolling into my life like she owns the damn place. I really hate that bitch.

Alzheimer's is mean and vindictive. She steals a little bit more from you each day, slowly, but surely, until you are left feeling empty and lost. Just when I begin to accept a new loss, Alzheimer's takes something else. It is a constant cycle of grief with her. She takes something from me. I grieve the loss. At some point, I finally begin to accept it. Then, she takes more. I'm on a continuous roller coaster of grief with her. When will she stop? When will she leave me alone? Only time will tell, I guess.

I often begin to think that I am doing a pretty good job of accepting my mom's Alzheimer's. I think that I have come to terms with our reality and that I am doing my best to deal with it. However, I've come to realize that it is all just part of the roller coaster ride with the mean girl in high school. At a time when I thought I had accepted Alzheimer's, she strolled into my life again one night in the form of a dream. Have you ever had a dream about something that just fucked you up for days? That's how this dream was for me. I dreamt that my mom was normal again. I dreamt that she didn't have Alzheimer's. The dream was as clear as day. I was at my mom's house and she told me that she had bought something for me while she was out shopping. I don't remember what it was that she had bought, but my mom used to do things like that all the time in real life. In the dream, she gave me this surprise gift and I could see how happy it made her to surprise me like that. She went on and on about how I could return it if I didn't like it, but I knew that I never would. That was pretty much it. It was a short dream, but it felt so real. I woke up feeling sad and missing her. Not necessarily missing her *now*, but missing her *then*. Trust me, there's a difference.

Anyway, I guess that bitch Alzheimer's had decided that it was time to start messing with me again because I wasn't able to stop thinking about that dream for weeks. I wasn't able to stop thinking about what my life would be like if my mom didn't have Alzheimer's. I honestly can't even begin to imagine it. In order to imagine it, I would have to be able to remember what she was like before she got Alzheimer's. But, I honestly can't remember sometimes. In the last almost six years, I have lost so much of her that I forget what she was like when she was whole. It's hard to remember her *then* because all I see is her *now*. Without a doubt, the hardest part of Alzheimer's is missing someone who is standing right in front of you. I want to love the mom I have now and I do, but I miss the mom I had then so, so much. I want to remember her, but it's hard because she's still here. She's just so different now. It's hard to focus on remembering someone when you are still focused on taking care of her. In my deepest, darkest, and most selfish moments, I wish that it was just over with already. I wish that I could speed up this whole process so that I could just be left alone with my grief and memories. So that I might actually be able to remember. It is not easy for me to admit that, but it's true. It's real.

Since having that dream, I have been making a real effort to remember my first mom, the one who raised me. Sometimes, I share these memories with my current mom and she tells me that she doesn't remember it. I tell her a lot of things about herself and she has a hard time believing them. She can't believe that she used to do my hair, clean her house, take me places, or even drive a car. She doesn't even remember that I used to live with her. How fucked up is that? It makes me sad. It makes me miss her. What I wouldn't give for just one day with my first mom. What I wouldn't give to make that bitch Alzheimer's go away for good. What I wouldn't give to just be able to remember what life was like before. My mom can't remember and I'm even starting to forget, but I'll do my best to remember her here.

Growing up, my mom used to dress me and my sister like twins. She would buy two of the same dress, one in purple for my sister and one in pink for me. I hate pink. She bought us all of the same toys, too. My mom bought us a present for everything. She bought us presents for Christmas, our birthdays, St. Patrick's Day, Valentine's Day, Easter, the end of the school year, the beginning of the school year, Halloween, and anything else she could think of. She often bought us gifts for no reason at all. We would come home from school one day to find a new outfit or a toy waiting for us on our beds. She did our hair every morning before school. She would make us sit on the toilet with the lid closed while she combed, pulled, yanked, and curled our hair to perfection. We would scream, "Owwww-aaaaa," and she would say, "He doesn't live here anymore!" She woke us up every morning by singing, "Rise and shine and give God your glory, glory! Rise and shine and give God your glory, glory! Rise and shine and give God your glory, glory! Children of Jerie." She volunteered and did lunch duty at our Catholic school any chance she got. She picked us up from school every day and often took us to get water ice on the way home. She probably chaperoned every field trip from the time I was in Pre-K to Eighth grade. She threw us a birthday party every year and let us have friends over whenever we wanted. She did anything and everything she could to make us happy. And, yes, she spoiled the crap out of us.

In high school, she took us back to school clothes shopping every year since we would no longer be wearing a uniform to school. She had us show her everything we tried on and we would put on a fashion show for her when we got home. She drove us anywhere and everywhere that we wanted to go, up until we got our driver's licenses. She took us to get our hair done all the time and she let me get highlights. She was there for me every day after school when I would cry about the girls who were harassing me. She listened every time I told her that one of them called me ugly or white trash or said that my boyfriend could do a lot better. She was there for me when they told everyone that I had herpes. She was there for me when they wrote shit about me on the bathroom walls. And, she gave me a high-five when I finally punched one of those girls in the face at lunch time, even though it got me suspended from school for two days. She let me transfer schools the next year. When I was 17, she found out that I had started smoking within days because she eavesdropped on my phone conversation with a friend. She had no shame in her eavesdropping game.

In college, she took me grocery shopping and did my laundry every time I came home. She sent me money all the time, even though she probably knew that I was spending it all on cigarettes and booze. She came up to my school and took me and my friends out to lunch on my birthday. She called me all the time when I was in class, even though I had printed out my schedule for her. She left me voice mails all the time, even though I told her not to. My sophomore year, she drove up to school, picked me up, took me home, and made me go vote. She didn't care that I had strep throat at the time. She told me that I ruined Christmas when I got a citation for underage drinking the night before I went home for winter break. When my driver's license got suspended as a result of that citation, she drove me everywhere again like she did before I turned 16. She paid all of my speeding and parking tickets and she always covered my bank fines when I overdrew on my account, which was a lot. She hated that I drank and partied so much, but she still answered the phone at 2am when I called her drunk and upset about my grandfather, who had recently passed away. She helped me move into and out of my dorm room every year. She helped me paint my room in the sorority house my senior year. And, she never complained about any of it. Not even once.

After college, she supported my dream of becoming a police officer and was there for me every step of the way. She understood when I didn't call her for a while because I was busy and worked different shifts. She didn't say anything when I practically moved in with my now-husband after our first date. She helped me find an apartment and stuff to go in it when I decided that I needed a break from living with my now-husband. Then, she helped me move back in with my now-husband when I decided that I was ready to do so. In my adult life, she probably helped me move about five times. She let me live my life the way I wanted to and she still supported me when it didn't work out. She still bought me gifts for any and every holiday she could think of. She still bought me gifts for no reason at all. One St. Patrick's Day, about a year before she was diagnosed, she made a big deal of having us all over to cook ham and cabbage to celebrate. She bought St. Patrick's Day decorations, plates, cups, and napkins. She bought each of us a St. Patrick's Day mug. She hated to cook and no one even liked ham and cabbage, so we all made fun of her a little bit. It makes me cry to think about it now. If I had known then that she would be diagnosed with Alzheimer's a year later, I would have eaten seconds and thirds without saying a word. What I wouldn't give for her to make me ham and cabbage now. I would eat it every day.

Well, that's all I've got for now. These memories are like my middle finger to Alzheimer's. Just like that mean girl in high school, she'll always come back to fuck with me some more. But, I'll always be here to punch her in the face and my mom will be waiting to give me a high-five. In case you haven't realized it yet, I have a pretty cool mom. She was cool then and she's still cool now. She's still my homegirl. Alzheimer's can't take that away from us. My mom might not be able to remember anymore, but that's ok. She might not be able to fight for herself, but that's ok, too. I'll remember for the both of us and I'll fight until the end. I'll fight by remembering. Alzheimer's is a mean girl, but you can't let the mean girls win.

What Is Alzheimer's?

Alzheimer's is asking the same question three times within ten minutes. It's telling someone the same information or story repeatedly. It's forgetting someone's name or the word for something. It's forgetting to do something that you were supposed to do, or forgetting that you already did it and doing it again.

Alzheimer's is forgetting how to fix your iced tea when you've been drinking it your whole life. It's forgetting what you usually order to eat at your favorite restaurant. It's missing the turn into your neighborhood, where you've lived for twenty years.

Alzheimer's is putting your shirt on backwards. It's putting your shoes on the wrong feet. It's wearing clothing that is inappropriate for the weather or the occasion. It's pairing a dressy blouse with a pair of sweatpants. It's forgetting how to dress altogether.

Alzheimer's is not wanting to take a shower or get dressed. It's forgetting how to put on your makeup and style your hair. It's using a black Sharpie marker to draw on your eyebrows instead of using an eyebrow pencil. It's brushing your teeth only once a day and washing your hair only once in a while. It's having a complete disregard for personal hygiene and your appearance, not because you don't care, but because you don't know any better.

Alzheimer's is slowly forgetting the details and memories of your own life. It's forgetting your loved ones and not being able to recognize them when you see them. It's thinking you haven't seen someone in a while, when you see them every day. It's thinking that you saw someone, when you only spoke to them on the phone.

Alzheimer's is forgetting where you grew up and where you went to school. It's forgetting your daughters' last names or what they do for a living. It's forgetting your daughters' graduations, weddings, and other important events. It's forgetting when your daughters were born. It's forgetting your own wedding. It's even forgetting how you met your own husband and when.

Alzheimer's is having a voice that you no longer know how to use. It's not being able to join in on a conversation or follow along with one. It's getting upset with your husband because you think he's ignoring you or not including you, but it's really that you are unable to participate.

Alzheimer's is having your adult daughter ask you if you have to use the bathroom before you go out and then helping you do so. It's having your adult daughter remind you to pull down both your pants and your underwear so that you don't pee through them again. It's having her remind you to throw the used toilet paper in the toilet or the trash, rather than balling it up and putting it in your pocket.

Alzheimer's is having a dirty, messy, cluttered house when it used to be spotless, immaculate, and organized. It's needing someone to show you around your own house, even though you've lived there for twenty-five years. It's watching someone else clean that house, not because you don't want to do it yourself, but because you don't know how to.

Alzheimer's is having tunnel vision so badly that you're practically blind. It's needing someone to hold your hand and guide you around everywhere you go. And, even then, you walk so slowly that it takes you forever to get anywhere. It's not being able to see something that's right in front of you, whether it's a pair of glasses on the kitchen counter or a huge ship passing by in the canal. It is thinking that you are walking up a step or over a curb when you are actually walking on flat ground. It's thinking that a rug on the floor is actually a hole in the floor.

Alzheimer's is needing someone to help you do almost everything, if not just simply doing it for you. It's forgetting how to walk, read, write, and even spell your own last name. It's losing everything you've learned, everything you know, and everything you have. It is becoming someone else that neither you nor your loved ones know.

Alzheimer's is a narcissistic thief that does not discriminate. It steals from the rich and the poor, the strong and the weak, the good and the bad. It does not care if you're black or white, male or female, young or old. It doesn't care if you have a little or a lot. It doesn't care if you're well educated or just plain dumb. Alzheimer's will rob you blind and you won't even know it.

Alzheimer's is a sick and twisted killer. It tortures its victims by causing an extremely slow, painful death. It laughs in the face of those who try to stop it by fighting for a cure. It doesn't care if you're a mother or a father, a sister or a brother, a husband or a wife. It has a complete disregard for your relationships with those around you. It will slowly kill you right before their eyes. It likes for them to watch. It doesn't care about the other battles that you may have already won or lost. It knows that your final battle will be against it and it knows that it will win.

My Life Today

A lot has happened in my life since I started writing this book. When I began writing it in April 2015, my husband, Steve, had just recently started his primary training in flight school. We were living at Fort Rucker, Alabama, with our two black labs, Oakley and Lucy. I was travelling home to Delaware about every two months or so to visit my parents.

In August 2015, my mom's mother, my Nan, became very sick and went into the hospital. Over the next three months, Nan went from the hospital to a rehabilitation center and back again several times. She never went home again. Nan entered end of life care in October 2015. She held on strong for a while, but she eventually passed away on November 19, 2015. I was unable to travel home to Delaware from Alabama for the funeral services. It absolutely tore me up inside. Making the situation even worse was the fact that I was unable to be there with my mom when she found out that her mom had died.

Initially, we weren't sure whether or not we should even tell my mom that her mom had died. Many people would argue that there is almost never a reason to tell an Alzheimer's patient that someone has died. However, in this case, my mom was extremely close to her mom, so we decided that we had to tell her. Even after she was diagnosed with Alzheimer's, my mom talked to Nan on the phone every single day. She had gone to visit Nan in the hospital and the rehab center several times during the three months that Nan was there. My mom absolutely remembered her mom and knew that she was very sick. My dad and my sister told my mom the news together. They told me that she cried a lot and she was very upset initially, but then she seemed to accept it. When I talked to my mom, she told me that Nan had died. She told me that she was upset at first, but that she had gotten over it. I knew then that although my mom had been very upset, she did not fully understand what it meant that her mom had died. She rarely ever spoke about Nan again after that. Even now, she only brings her up once in a while and it is clear to me that she doesn't fully understand what happened. But, that's probably a good thing. After Nan died, I began to feel like I was ready to move back home.

Steve and I spent Christmas 2015 in Alabama. I was a little sad that we weren't spending it with our families, but we had a lot to get done before moving back to Delaware. Steve graduated flight school on January 21, 2016. We moved home a few days later in the middle of a blizzard. We arrived home to two feet of snow on the ground. It didn't take long for the snow to melt and for us to get settled back into our home in Delaware. Steve quickly began flying for his National Guard unit and went back to work at the police department shortly after.

Once we were settled in and back into our routine, I continued writing my book. I also went back to being a part-time caregiver for my mom. I go to her house about two or three times a week to take care of her while my dad goes to work. I have begun doing different activities with her, such as laundry, housework, crafts, spelling bees, trips to the park, walks, picnics, etc. I am doing my best to navigate my way through this storm. I have already learned so much, but I am hoping to continue to learn more along the way.

Currently, we are working on trying to convince my dad to finally retire from his job. We would also like to convince him to hire full-time professional in-home help for my mom. As hard as it is for me to admit this, my dad is still leaving my mom home alone for a few hours on days that I don't come over, so that he can go to work. He doesn't go to work every day and when he does, it's only for a few hours at a time, but that is still too much. I personally have struggled with this situation a lot. It angers and upsets me that my dad is still leaving my mom home alone in her condition. I go over to their house about twice a week to take care of my mom while my dad is at work, but it pains me to think that she is being left alone on the days that I am not there. My dad is hesitant to hire a caregiver because he does not think that my mom will like it. He also has a very difficult time asking for help. He always feels like he needs to do everything on his own and carry the full weight of things on his own shoulders. As mad and upset as I get over this situation, I try to remind myself that my dad is doing the best he can. He doesn't really know what to do or how to handle many situations, as we are all just learning how to weather this storm as we go.

When my dad leaves my mom home alone, she generally just sits in front of the television the entire time that he is gone. I don't even want to think about all of the possibilities of things that could happen to her while she is home all by herself. She can no longer take care of herself and she can no longer use the phone, so she wouldn't even be able to call anyone if she needed help. Even when my dad is home, my mom still tends to spend most of her time sitting in front of the television. She often tells me that she is bored. I know that my dad is having an extremely difficult time accepting and dealing with my mom's Alzheimer's. Many times, it is just easier for him to ignore my mom than it is to try to deal with her. It makes me sad and angry sometimes, but again, I try to remind myself that my dad is doing the best he can. I know that he is stressed out, overwhelmed, miserable, and depressed. But, I don't know what else I can do to help him. He has to be willing to help himself by hiring a professional caregiver. I'm hoping that will happen one day in the near future.

In the meantime, I try to make the most of my time with my mom. I try to make up for all the time that she is just sitting in front of the television, bored out of her mind. I try to do a new activity with her each time I go over to her house. Sometimes we do laundry and clean a little bit. Sometimes we do fun, easy crafts, play with Play-doh, or go to the park. Other times we just listen to Elvis and, if I'm lucky, I can get her up and dancing around a little bit. I definitely think that the more time she spends sitting in front of the television, the worse her symptoms become. She is always more confused and has a much more difficult time getting up to do things. She has no concept of time so all of her days just blend together, especially when she sits in front of the television day after day. She needs to be mentally stimulated and physically active as much as possible. I feel that when she is being engaged and interacted with, she comes alive and her symptoms seem to diminish, if even just slightly. There are still times when she is really able to connect. I know that her Alzheimer's will never be cured. It will never go away and she will continue to have bad days. But, there's no reason why I can't try to outnumber the bad days with good ones. To try to get ahead of the storm. On the days that I visit with her and interact with her, she always tells my dad that she had a really good day. So, fuck you Alzheimer's! I must be doing something right.

I have struggled with many things since my mom was diagnosed with Alzheimer's. I have been consumed with guilt and regret. I have often times misplaced my patience and my strength. I have struggled with learning to love the stranger that my mom has become. I have resented family members and friends for not helping out more, even though I understand that everyone has a life to live. I have resented people my age who complain about their parents for stupid reasons. Well, they seem like stupid reasons to me, but I also understand that it is all a matter of perspective. I have also been jealous of people my age, or any age really, who have a great relationship with their parents, as I feel as though I have been robbed of that opportunity. I have struggled with the never-ending cycle of grief, as I grieve my parents even though they are both still alive. Neither one of them will ever be the same again. Alzheimer's has taken so much from both of them and has left me and my sister to take care of both of our parents now. Finally, I have struggled with allowing myself to continue living my own life in spite of my mom's Alzheimer's. I still have a hard time separating my life as a caregiver from my life as Lauren. I know that I still deserve to have my own life, but it's hard to do that sometimes.

I have also learned a lot along the way. I have learned to stop feeling sorry for myself, which has allowed me to find my strength. I have learned to lower my expectations of my mom and our time together. I have learned that it is okay to have regrets. I have learned that in order to focus on what is truly important, I must free myself of all the negativity, drama, and toxic people in my life. Most importantly, I have learned that my mom is still Jerie. She still deserves love and attention. She still deserves to be happy. As long as she's happy, then that's all that matters. I have also learned that my mom is probably more afraid and frustrated than I am. She knows that something is happening to her. Nothing is worth making her upset, scared, or embarrassed. Nothing. She needs and deserves to be reassured and guided through the rest of her days, each and every one of them. She deserves for me to take care of her the way she once took care of me. It's the least I can do. When I put myself in her shoes and try to imagine how she must feel, I realize that none of this is about me. It's all about her. And if I were her, I would want someone to give me a chance. I would want someone to take care of me and to make me feel safe. So, that is my number one goal.

I have also learned a few practical things and techniques that can be used every day. I have learned to speak slowly and simply, always one person at a time. Never argue or correct her. If she says that something didn't happen, then it didn't happen. Never ask her if she remembers something, but instead remind her of the things she has forgotten. If she says or does something wrong, it's usually not a big deal, so there is no need to correct her. I have learned to let things go. Nothing is worth making her upset or embarrassed. Distraction and redirection are key when she is confused, upset, or repeating herself. I can almost always find a way to distract her and redirect her attention to something else in order to prevent her from getting upset about something. Distraction and redirection also help to keep me sane when she is constantly repeating the same stories or asking me the same questions. I have learned that it is always easier to simply take her hand and guide her somewhere than it is to try to tell her where to go or what to do. I have also learned that although she can't see very well or understand very much, she can touch and feel, so I let her. She can especially feel or sense emotions, so I try to never get angry or upset in front of her. Ever. She can also feel love, so I love her.

Without a doubt, the most important thing that I have learned is that just because there's no treatment and no cure, it does not mean that you have to take this disease lying down. It doesn't mean that you can't still fight for your life. Maybe it's not just about finding a cure, but about creating a life full of precious memories. Maybe it's not a life sentence, but a sentence to live your life. A chance to make the most out of your life and your time with your loved ones. A chance to make memories, no matter how big or how small. A chance to enjoy living in spite of the disease. It forces you to open your eyes and to truly appreciate your loved ones. You learn not to take a single thing for granted.

After my mom's diagnosis, I was angry and sad for a very long time. I wasted a lot of time feeling sorry for myself. I eventually learned how to stop and smell the roses. I learned how to live in the moment. I learned to cherish the good times with my mom because they are often few and far between. I learned that it is possible to improve the quality of life for someone who has Alzheimer's. That's what's more important. You can do more than just sit there and watch your loved one slowly die. Engage them. Interact with them. Take time to do fun activities with them and be patient with them when they have difficulty doing these activities. My mom might have Alzheimer's, but I can still create moments of joy in her life. I can pay attention to her and take advantage of the times when she is really able to connect. Alzheimer's will eventually take her life, but I can give her a good life while she is still her.

I'm not going to lie. It's hard. It's always going to be hard. Alzheimer's is a horrible, fucked up, inhumane disease. We should absolutely keep fighting to find a cure. But, I urge you not to give up on your life in doing so. Don't sit around waiting for a cure. Chances are that if you or your loved one already has the disease, it's too late for you anyway. *Live your life*. Find joy in simple things. Continue to make memories even if they will be forgotten. Don't sit around waiting for the storm to pass. Learn to dance in the rain. Learn to weather the storm.

To be continued…

About the Author

Lauren Dykovitz lives in Delaware with her husband, Steve, and her two black labs, Oakey and Lucy. Her mom, Jerie, is still living with Alzheimer's disease. She is now 69-years-old.

This is Lauren's first book. She hopes that it will be the first of many, as she plans to continue sharing her story and all that she learns along the way. Please check out her blog at thelaurendykovitzblog.wordpress.com for more of Lauren's work.

Please visit the Alzheimer's Association website at alz.org for more information and to find out how you can join the fight to end Alzheimer's.

34069339R00148

Made in the USA
Lexington, KY
18 March 2019